X-PLANES 9

DORNIER Do 335

Robert Forsyth

SERIES EDITOR TONY HOLMES

OSPREY
PUBLISHING

OSPREY PUBLISHING
Bloomsbury Publishing Plc

Kemp House, Chawley Park, Cumnor Hill, Oxford OX2 9PH, UK
29 Earlsfort Terrace, Dublin 2, Ireland
1385 Broadway, 5th Floor, New York, NY 10018, USA
Email: info@ospreypublishing.com
www.ospreypublishing.com

OSPREY is a trademark of Osprey Publishing Ltd

First published in Great Britain in 2018
Transferred to digital print in 2023

© Osprey Publishing Ltd, 2018

A catalog record for this book is available from the British Library.

Print ISBN: 978 1 4728 2889 7
ePub: 978 1 4728 2898 9
ePDF: 978 1 4728 2899 6
XML: 978 1 4728 2900 9

Edited by Tony Holmes
Cutaway and cockpit by Adam Tooby
Battlescene and cover artwork by Wiek Luijken
Three-view artwork by Simon Schatz
Index by Mark Swift
Typeset by PDQ Digital Media Solutions, Bungay, UK
Printed and bound in India by Replika Press Private Ltd.

MIX
Paper from
responsible sources
FSC® C016779
www.fsc.org

23 24 25 26 27   10 9 8 7 6 5 4 3

The Woodland Trust
Osprey Publishing supports the Woodland Trust, the UK's leading woodland
conservation charity.

www.ospreypublishing.com
To find out more about our authors and books visit our website. Here you
will find extracts, author interviews, details of forthcoming events and the
option to sign-up for our newsletter.

Acknowledgements
The author would like to extend his
thanks to J. Richard Smith and
Eddie J. Creek for their kind
assistance during the writing of this
book. For those readers wishing to
delve deeper into the history of the
extraordinary Dornier Do 335, they are
recommended to read Richard's and
Eddie's *Dornier Do 335 Pfeil/Arrow*
(Crécy Publishing, Manchester, 2017).
I am also grateful, as ever, to Ted
Oliver for kindly offering his expertise.

Front Cover
What could have been … Wiek
Luijken's dramatic illustration depicts
the moment a Do 335A-6 nightfighter
of the *Stab* IV./NJG 3 based at
Nordholz passes close by its victim,
a burning Lancaster bomber – one of
a formation out to bomb naval targets
in the Bremerhaven area on a moonlit
night in the autumn of 1946. The
Do 335A-6 is fitted with flame
dampers and has a small glazed panel
that was faired into the upper
fuselage, aft of the pilot and directly
above the accommodation, intended
for a second crewmember/radar
operator. The dipole aerials for the
FuG 218 Neptun SN-2 radar can be
seen extending above and below each
wing. The aircraft, which has two
20mm cannon mounted in the nose
above the forward engine, is finished
in a typical RLM 76/75 mottled
nightfighter scheme on the
uppersurfaces, while the
undersurfaces are 76.

XPLANES

CONTENTS

CHAPTER ONE

INTRODUCTION

It was in the summer of 1945 that the highly experienced British naval test pilot Lt Cdr Eric 'Winkle' Brown, assigned to the Experimental Flying Detachment at Royal Aircraft Establishment (RAE) Farnborough, first saw the Dornier Do 335. This enormous aircraft, which the Germans called, oddly, the *Pfeil* (Arrow), bemused him. Years after the war, he recalled it being 'a quite remarkable and distinctly bizarre creation'. Like most observers, he felt that, 'Few aircraft could have possessed more remote a resemblance to a slender, pointed missile, but if hardly arrow-shaped and if aesthetically one of the least attractive fighters of its generation, it was certainly one of the fastest piston-engined fighters in the world.' And that was the point. The Do 335, through its two Daimler-Benz DB 603 engines rated at 1,750hp at takeoff, had power and pace – both increasingly important tactical attributes.

By 1942, all sides in the global air war were clear that modern aircraft needed a challenging combination of speed and firepower, which was something that was generally only attainable through lightness of airframe and/or from powerful engines. In this regard, most of the major warring nations were perfecting winning designs. In Britain, the Supermarine Spitfire had proved itself a superlative combat aircraft in 1940, and in 1942 the all-wood, twin-engined de Havilland Mosquito burst into the arena, giving the Allies an exceptionally fast, multi-role aircraft. In the United States, the North American P-51 Mustang had entered service, and while fitted with the Allison V-1710-39 engine for deployment with the RAF, it was laying the foundations for an aircraft that would have unprecedented

Do 335A-0 Wk-Nr 240107 VG+PM, parked on the rain-slick concrete at Oberpfaffenhofen in December 1944. An ungainly but intriguing aircraft, the Do 335's unusual design and power system gave it almost unrivalled speed, but this came with complex and often unreliable engineering.

range, speed and manoeuvrability once examples powered by the Rolls-Royce Merlin engine reached the USAAF in late 1943.

In the Third Reich, much work had been undertaken by the firms of Heinkel and Messerschmitt into the areas of jet and rocket propulsion. In March 1941 the world's first jet-powered aircraft (intended as a fighter), the Heinkel He 280, had taken to the air under its own power. Just over a year later, on 18 July 1942, the Messerschmitt Me 262 flew for the first time, powered by Junkers Jumo 004 jet engines. War had drastically hastened technical innovation in the air.

Most of Western Europe was firmly under German occupation. In one form or another, Hitler's 'Thousand-Year Reich' spread from Norway to the French Riviera, from the Channel coast to Czechoslovakia. But, militarily, by mid-1942, Nazi Germany was at a precipitous stage in its existence. Its conquest of Russia extended deep into Ukraine, reaching towards Rostov-on-Don, but, worryingly, in North Africa, Generalfeldmarschall Erwin Rommel's advance towards Cairo had ground to a halt. With just 55 functioning tanks, his *Afrika Korps* was stopped at a place called El Alamein, where British and Commonwealth troops held the ground, being kept replenished with American supplies.

It was in the air, however, that things had begun to appear particularly ominous. On the night of 30/31 May 1942, the RAF carried out a night raid on the city of Cologne in which 890 bombers had dropped more than 1,450 tons of bombs on the city, killing 469 of its residents and injuring 5,027. More than 12,000 buildings were affected in some way by the raid, and water and electricity supplies, telephone communication and mail were inoperative or disrupted for two weeks. Yet, the nature of the air war over Europe changed indelibly still further when, in the late afternoon of 17 August, 12 USAAF four-engine B-17 Flying Fortress 'heavy' bombers escorted by four squadrons of RAF Spitfires targeted the marshalling yards at Sotteville, near Rouen in France, dropping 18 tons of bombs. Throughout the rest of August, the Americans launched more tentative daylight raids with their bombers on marshalling yards, shipyards and airfields.

As a result of shifting dynamics in the war, which was being fought at ever greater distances, and with the appearance of large four-engine Allied bombers over the Reich, the Luftwaffe required adaptable aircraft designs that were capable of fulfilling, amongst other things, the role of a new generation of high-speed bomber, possibly to improve on the Ju 88. Such aircraft were needed to render support to the land-based campaigns in the East, whilst also being able to perform as long-range maritime bomber and reconnaissance aircraft in the campaign over the Atlantic where Admiral Karl Dönitz needed air support for his U-boats. Then there was the *Reichsverteidigung* – the day and night air defence of the German homeland – where fighters were needed that possessed speed and range to tackle Allied daylight and night bombing raids, but which were able to carry sufficient armament, munitions, technical equipment (such as radar) and fuel loads without any compromise to performance.

To use contemporary parlance, this was a 'big ask'. Nevertheless, in 1942 the RLM (*Reichsluftministerium* – German Air Ministry) issued an official requirement for a twin-engine *Schnellbomber* – effectively a fast fighter-bomber – capable of carrying a 500kg bomb at speeds of around 800km/h over a distance of 2,000km. The specification was issued to the firms of Arado, Junkers, Messerschmitt and, eventually, Dornier.

The first three of these manufacturers had submitted their design proposals for consideration at a preliminary meeting held at the RLM on 12 December 1942. Arado offered the E 561, a project based on a twin radial-engined design with twin tail fins that incorporated a gearing system to allow power to be distributed equally between the propellers in the eventuality that one engine failed. The proposed Junkers EF 115 was a low-wing monoplane, mounted on a tricycle undercarriage and powered by two engines, one of which was installed in the nose and the other in the fuselage behind the cockpit, which had an all-round vision canopy. The rear engine drove a co-axial contra-rotating propeller by means of an extension shaft.

The Messerschmitt contender was the Bf 109Z ('*Zwilling*' – twin) in which two Bf 109Fs were mated by a central wing section and horizontal stabilizer. The cockpit of the right-side fuselage was to be removed and faired over, the space gained being used for fuel, while the pilot would occupy the left side. The aircraft would be powered by two Daimler-Benz DB 605 engines and armed with either five 30mm cannon or carry a 1,000kg bomb load.

When Dr.-Ing. Claudius Dornier, the founder of the Dornier Flugzeugwerke, was informed of the RLM requirement, he complained to the ministry over the initial exclusion of his company in the tender process. This was most likely attributable to the fact that the thought among senior figures within the RLM was that Dornier should be left to continue and concentrate on production of bomber/twin-engine aircraft (i.e., the Do 217) and seaplanes. One RLM official is reputed to have scoffed, 'Dornier is only good enough to build conventional bombers. What does he know about fighters?' However, Dornier's representations were vocal enough to cause a shift in the RLM's viewpoint, and the Bavarian designer knew just the project that he would submit to the ministry.

CHAPTER TWO

ORIGINS

Göppingen Gö 9 D-EBYW filmed during a test flight, the aircraft having been towed into the air by a Do 17. Such tests assisted Claude Dornier in his work on the P.59 project.

Claude Dornier was born on 14 May 1884 in the ancient Swabian town of Kempten im Allgäu. His father was French and imported wine, his mother German. In 1907, at the age of 23, he graduated as a mechanical engineer from the Technical University of Munich and three years later joined the experimental design office of the airship manufacturer Luftschiffbau Zeppelin at the company's Friedrichshafen works following a brief spell employed in the Nagel Engineering Works, a steel company in Karlsruhe.

Dornier was a creative young man. During his formative time with Zeppelin, amongst other things, he designed a revolving hangar suitable for the company's huge airships. *Graf* Ferdinand von Zeppelin was so impressed by the young engineer that he asked him to work specifically on the design of heavier-than-air, metal aircraft at a new facility of the Zeppelin Werke at Lindau-Reutin. Here, Dornier focused on ascertaining the practicalities of using light metals in aircraft construction, and he was responsible for the emergence of a series of large, multi-engined flying boats. Also appearing during World War I were the Zeppelin-Lindau C I and C II two-seat, biplane ground-attack aircraft, completed in response to a requirement from the *Luftstreitkräfte*. A series of nine C Is was produced, the prototype making its first flight in early March 1917. The C II, which differed in the design of its radiator, failed to meet the performance criteria when tested on 18 March 1918.

An all-metal biplane fighter, the D I, was built with stressed fuselage skinning of Duralumin and was seen as a successor to the Fokker D VII. One example of a D I was test-flown on 3 July 1918 by a certain Oberleutnant Hermann Göring, the commander of *Jasta* 27, at the Adlershof fighter competition, despite the aircraft having not yet passed its official construction and delivery checks. Following Göring's flight, he handed the D I over to Hauptmann Wilhelm Reinhard, the commander of *Jagdgeschwader* I, but the aircraft suffered the loss of its top wing as it came out of a steep dive and Reinhard, a 20-victory ace, was killed.

The crash of the D I seems to have done little to arrest Dornier's career. After World War I, Dornier focused once more on building flying boats from a new base in Friedrichshafen. Known by 1923 as the Dornier Flugzeugwerke, the company had acquired the manufacturing facilities of the Flugzeugbau Friedrichshafen and embarked upon the design and construction of a somewhat ungainly series of commercial flying boats with the engines mounted on either the top of the wing or directly above the nose. One such machine, the Dornier L 1 *Delphin* (Dolphin) was sold to the US Navy, while the L 2 went to Japan. These machines were powered variously by BMW III or IV, Rolls-Royce Falcon or Isotta Fraschini A10 engines. Another series of two-seater, parasol wing flying boats was assigned the name *Libelle* (Dragonfly), with the prototype *Libelle* I, of what would be a series of five such aircraft, making its first flight on 16 August 1921 powered by a Siemens SH 5 five-cylinder radial engine. The following *Libelle* II was longer and heavier and powered by the Sh 11 engine, of which five examples are believed to have been completed, one going to Brazil.

Dornier persisted with this rather unattractive design style in what was effectively a land variant of the *Delphin* in what became known as the Dornier C III *Komet* I, although the inclusion of a fixed undercarriage meant that the 185hp BMW IIIa engine could be mounted in line with the fuselage rather than on top of the nose or wing. Similarly, the Dornier *Spatz* (Sparrow) was a landplane version of the *Libelle*, while the Dornier H *Falke* (Falcon) was intended as a monoplane fighter based on the Zeppelin-Lindau D I in which the pilot was accommodated in an open cockpit immediately behind the centre of the trailing edge of the high wing. This aircraft flew for the first time on 1 November 1922, but did not enter production, although the airframe was converted for maritime use with twin floats and known as the *Seefalke* (Seafalcon).

That same year, the design office of the Dornier company was briefly closed by the Allied Control Commission. Although military development was forbidden by the Control Commission until 1926, this did not prevent Dornier from establishing a subsidiary in Italy at Marina di Pisa as the *Societa di Construzioni Meccaniche Aeronautiche* (CMASA). This operation was intended specifically to build a development of the prohibited Gs II flying boat. Later known as the Dornier J *Wal* (Whale), the sleek-hulled CMASA-built prototype, with

Professor Claude Honoré Desiré Dornier believed fervently in the alternative twin-engined power system concept that he eventually incorporated into the Do 335. As an aircraft designer, he had proved his capabilities for more than 20 years, being responsible for a range of successful seaplanes and early all-metal aircraft. During the war, Dornier also gained the faith of influential figures such as Erhard Milch. (Photo by Keystone-France/Gamma-Keystone via Getty Images)

its single engine mounted atop its wing, flew on 6 November 1922 and proved such a success that the majority of the shares in the Italian subsidiary were transferred to an Italian syndicate to finance immediate tooling for its series production. No fewer than 20 world records would be set by the *Wal*.

However, the design that would perhaps have the greatest effect on Dornier's career profile was the Do X, a massive new flying boat which was scheduled to make its maiden flight from the company's new works at Altenrhein, on the southern side of the Bodensee, in Switzerland, in July 1929. The all-metal, 12-engined Do X passenger '*Flugschiff*' ('flying ship') had been conceived by Dornier as a means of crossing what were deemed to be the 'uncrossable' oceans of the world, particularly the Atlantic, so as to open up new inter-continental transport links. Powered by 12 525hp Bristol Jupiter nine-cylinder radials, the vast, 40m-long Do X, with its wingspan of 48m, was designed to carry around 70 passengers and a crew of 14 over a distance of 2,200km, together with luggage, freight and supplies. The aircraft was to be fitted with a bar, a ventilated smoking room with eight leather armchairs, a convertible four-berth sleeping compartment, a conference room and a large passenger saloon. There was also to be an electrically equipped kitchen and toilet and washroom compartments. The Do X represented a new dawn in luxury air travel, but to comply with the Versailles Treaty, Dornier had had to build his new, state-of-the-art machine on Swiss soil.

Progress on the Do X had proceeded sufficiently for the aircraft to make its maiden flight on the morning of 12 July. After a quick roll-out down the slipway, engine run-ups and water trials, the huge aircraft took to the air with no fewer than 16 people on board plus equipment, representing an all-up weight of 35 tonnes. Airborne for barely two-and-a-half minutes at less than five metres above the water, the Dornier touched back down on the surface and followed this with two more takeoffs before returning to its docking yard. One observer described events as follows:

'Dr Dornier, amid enthusiastic cheers and handshaking, climbs aboard the Do X. The crowds rejoice. Finally, the flying boat is taken in tow and anchored to the buoy. People congratulate Dr Dornier and his colleagues, shake their hands and rejoice with them.'

Despite delays and damage to its wing along the way, the aircraft arrived in New York on a publicity trip on 27 August 1931, having flown via England, the Canary Islands, Portuguese Guinea, Brazil and the West Indies. However, the aircraft failed to attract potential buyers and remained in New York for nine months before returning to Germany in May 1932.

After the rise of Adolf Hitler in Germany in early 1933, Dornier continued to focus his skills on the design of large, multi-engine bombers. To a great extent this design focus was aided and driven by the doctrinal beliefs of, from 1935, the new Luftwaffe's Chief of Staff, Oberst Walther Wever, who reasoned that Germany would need a large, multi-engined bomber to spearhead its strategy in any future war. Geopolitical factors meant that targets for such an aircraft could lie east

of the Ural Mountains, deep in the Soviet Union. Wever thus issued a specification to the Junkers and Dornier firms for what he termed a 'Ural Bomber', capable of carrying a heavy load of ordnance over a long range, but at speed and equipped with sufficient defensive armament.

Dornier's submission was the Do 19, a large, four-engined, box-like, mid-wing monoplane with twin tailfins, designed originally to carry no fewer than six gunners. Underpowered for its size and weight, it was to be fitted initially with nine-cylinder, 715hp air-cooled Bramo 322 H-2 radial engines, generating a maximum speed of only 370km/h over a maximum range of 1,995km with a bomb load of 1,600kg. The aircraft had a crew of nine and was armed with two 7.9mm MG 15 machine guns and two 20mm MG FF cannon. The first and only prototype to be completed, the V1 first flew on 28 October 1936 with the Bramo powerplants, but both the V2 (enhanced by the planned installation of more powerful BMW 132F nine-cylinder radials) and the V3 (with two 20mm cannon housed in two two-man hydraulically powered turrets and two machine guns in nose and tail positions) were scrapped prior to their completion.

The Do 19 was actually the latest in a line of Dornier heavy bombers, stretching back to the three-engined Dornier Y, or Do 15, a shoulder-wing monoplane, powered by three 450hp Bristol Jupiter engines – two in the wings and the third positioned above the centre section on struts. The Do 15 prototype flew for the first time on 17 October 1931, with some subsequent examples going to Yugoslavia. The Do F (or Do 11) was a slab-sided, twin-engined, high-wing monoplane capable of carrying a 1,000kg bombload, with examples being delivered to the *Fliegergruppen* at Merseburg and Fassberg – some of the Luftwaffe's earliest units. It suffered from undercarriage retraction

Clad in their Kapok life vests, the crew of what is believed to be Major Rudolf Gabelmann's Do 17Z of the Erg.St./KG 3 appear relieved to have safely returned to base following a mission in late 1940 or early 1941. Claude Dornier's most famous design, the Do 17 was originally conceived as a high-speed mailplane. However, it saw service as a bomber and reconnaissance aircraft with the Luftwaffe from the Spanish Civil War, throughout the early German campaigns in Poland, the West and the Balkans to the invasion of the USSR. The aircraft seen here appears to have had black distemper applied crudely to its undersides (as had other aircraft of the unit), suggesting deployment in night operations.

problems, however, and these led to the experimental Do 13 being built with fixed gear. Some Do 11s were operated by Lufthansa on behalf of the German State Railways, flying the Berlin–Königsberg route amongst others.

The Do 23 was, in essence, a progression of the Do 13. Featuring a more robustly built airframe and a reduced wingspan, it was initially powered by two 690hp BMW VI d engines – later versions were fitted with a pair of 750hp BMW VI u motors. A series of 200 machines was produced, with some being taken on by the bomber units I./KG 152, II./KG 153 and II./KG 252.

Aside from bombers, Dornier maintained its output of flying boats. In this regard, the sole example of the Do 14, an experimental long-range flying boat built in 1936, has some relevance to this story in that this design featured a pair of BMW VI engines built into the hull, but with a shaft driving a pusher propeller mounted above the wing by means of a complex gearbox.

However, the type that was to cement Dornier's reputation as one of Germany's foremost aircraft designers and manufacturers had first been developed back in 1932. Despite originating from a specification from the *Heereswaffenamt* (Army Ordnance Office), the Do 17 had been designed as a passenger/mailplane from the start and was intended to serve on Lufthansa's fast domestic and inter-European routes. The prototype, which had flown for the first time on 20 November 1934, took the form of a shoulder-wing monoplane with a very slim fuselage. It was powered by two 660hp BMW VI engines, and while its performance was excellent, internally it was extremely cramped, with very little space for its six passengers.

The aircraft was rejected by Lufthansa, but thanks to the efforts of Flugkapitän Robert Untucht, it found alternative employment as a high-speed bomber. The Do 17E bomber, which would gain international fame as the '*Fliegender Bleistift*' ('Flying Pencil'), carried a crew of three and was powered by a pair of 750hp BMW VI engines that gave it a maximum speed of 355km/h. The offensive load was limited to 500kg of bombs, with defensive armament being provided by two MG 15 machine guns. The type entered Luftwaffe service with KG 153 and KG 155 during the spring of 1937 and went on to see combat with the *Legion Condor* during the Spanish Civil War. The improved Do 17Z variant was widely used during the invasion of Poland in September 1939, throughout the campaign in the West in 1940 and in the ill-fated offensive against Britain during the summer and autumn of that same year. The long, 'pencil'-thin Do 17 was used as a bomber (by KGs 2, 3, 76 and 77) and reconnaissance aircraft, and later several Z-7 and Z-10 '*Kauz*' nightfighter variants were operated by NJGs 1 and 2.

A derivative of the Do 17, the Do 215 underwent engine progression from Gnome-Rhône radials to Daimler-Benz inlines and was put into series production for the Swedish Air Force in 1939, but this order for 18 machines was halted in August of that year because of gathering war clouds, as was an order from Yugoslavia. The Do 215 was, however, exported to Hungary and two were acquired by the Soviet Union.

The Luftwaffe used the aircraft for clandestine reconnaissance flights over Russia by the *Aufklärungsgruppe* Ob.d.L. and, as the Do 215B-5, as a nightfighter with NJGs 1 and 2, while several senior Luftwaffe commanders, such as Generalfeldmarschall Albert Kesselring, would utilise it as personal transport.

But as early as 1937, Dornier had proposed another design which was, in effect, a larger version of the Do 17. The Do 217 would prove to be a successful frontline aircraft for both the company and the Luftwaffe, with the first prototype taking to the air in August 1938. After a run of prototype-testing, the engine arrangement finally settled on was two 1,550hp BMW 801s. The first Do 217 variant to see operational service with the Luftwaffe was the E-model, which was taken on strength for reconnaissance missions by 3.(F)/11 operating from Rumania in late 1940 on mapping flights over the Soviet Union. The first bomber unit to be equipped with the Do 217 was II./KG 40 in March 1941, based initially at Lüneburg before moving to Cognac, from where the *Gruppe* undertook anti-shipping operations over the Atlantic. The type would remain assigned to II. *Gruppe* until 1943, when it was replaced by the He 177. More Do 217s were assigned to the *Geschwaderstab* and I./KG 2 at Achmer and Rheine in August 1941, then II. *Gruppe* at Évreux and, from September 1942, III./KG 2 at Achmer.

Between 1939 and 1941, alongside the development and acceptance by the Luftwaffe of the Do 17, Do 215 and Do 217 bomber and reconnaissance types, Dornier continued to establish itself as a major supplier of maritime aircraft. Indeed, between 1935 and 1940, no fewer than 170 single-engined Do 18 flying boats had been built in three Dornier factories. Despite the type's obsolescence by the outbreak of World War II, 62 examples remained in frontline use with four *Küstenfliegergruppe Staffeln* well into 1940. During the campaign against Britain in the summer of that year, only 2./Kü.Fl.Gr. 106 was operational with the type on the Channel Front, however.

Another mainstay flying boat for the Luftwaffe was the graceful, three-engined Do 24, which had first flown in July 1937 and had its origins in a Dutch naval requirement for a replacement for the Dornier *Wal*. This 22m-long aircraft featured a high wing, onto which all three (initially) 600hp Junkers Jumo 205C diesel engines, then BMW-Bramo 323R-2 *Fafnir* radial engines, were mounted. The wing was given extra support by struts fitted to sponsons extending from the centre fuselage. Although designed by the Dornier Flugzeugwerke, most ensuing Do 24s were built in the occupied Netherlands and France, as well as by the Weser Flugzeugbau near Bremen. In Luftwaffe service, the Do 24 served mainly with the *Seenotdienst* (air-sea rescue), but also with *Transport* and *Küstenfliegerstaffeln*.

However, while Dornier, through its various companies and design offices, may have been prolific, it was in August 1937 that Dr.-Ing. Claude Dornier had filed a patent for an 'Airframe for Aircraft with power propulsions' – the plural of 'propulsions' being the key word here. Ever since his early involvement with Zeppelin, Dornier had championed designs which incorporated back-to-back engine

OPPOSITE
One of Dornier's most successful inter-war seaplane designs was the graceful Do 18. This Dornier-Werke advertisement shows Do 18E Wk-Nr 661 D-ABYM *Aeolus*, which, after trials with the *Erprobungsstelle* Travemünde, was used by Deutsche Lufthansa on its South Atlantic mail service from Bathurst, in The Gambia, to Natal, in Brazil. The aircraft was lost, however, on 30 July 1937 after suffering engine problems and being damaged during an attempted retrieval operation at sea.

BETRIEBSSTOFFANLAGE:

In zwei benzindichten Schotträumen in den Flossenstummeln können 1800 l Betriebsstoff und in den 4 Aluminiumbehältern des Kraftstoffraums 2120 l Betriebsstoff mitgeführt werden.

FUELLING SYSTEM:

The fueltight bulkhead compartments in the lateral fins carry 1800 litres of fuel, whilst the 4 aluminium tanks in the fuel compartment have a capacity of 2120 litres.

LANGSTRECKENFLUGBOOT DORNIER DO 18
LONG-DISTANCE FLYING BOAT DORNIER DO 18

TECHNISCHE DATEN:	Do 18 E	Do 18 F	TECHNICAL DATA:	Do 18 E	Do 18 F
Spannweite	23,70 m	26,30 m	Span	23.70 m.	26.30 m.
Flügelfläche	98,00 m²	111,20 m²	Wing area	98.00 sq. m.	111.20 sq. m.
Größte Länge	19,25 m	19,25 m	Overall length . . .	19.25 m.	19.25 m.
Größte Höhe . . .	5,45 m	5,40 m	Overall height . . .	5.45 m.	5.40 m.
Fluggewicht	10 000 kg	11 000 kg	Flying weight . . .	10 000 kgs.	11 000 kgs.
Höchstgeschwindigkeit .	260 km/st	250 km/st	Maximum speed . .	260 km. p. hr.	250 km. p. hr.
Gipfelhöhe	4 500 m	5 600 m	Ceiling	4 500 m.	5 600 m.
Landegeschwindigkeit .	90 km/st	85 km/st	Landing speed . . .	90 km. p. hr.	85 km. p. hr.
Reisegeschwindigkeit .	225 km/st	220 km/st	Cruising speed . . .	225 km. p. hr.	220 km. p. hr.
Größter Flugbereich . . .	8 500 km	über 8 500 km	Radius of action . .	8 500 km.	over 8 500 km.

Do 18

arrangements, driving both tractor and pusher propellers, for example, and as mentioned, the Do 14 flying boat. His all-metal Rs I biplane flying boat of 1915, which was the first German aircraft to be covered entirely in stressed Duralumin, was powered by three 240hp Maybach engines arranged to drive large pusher propellers, although the aircraft was wrecked in a storm before flight trials could begin.

Dornier's 1937 patent applied the same fundamental design but, secretly, for a fighter aircraft. The patent described the aircraft as 'consisting of at least three separately built and interchangeable parts, i.e., front section containing a propulsion unit with tractor propeller, a centre section protected by firewalls fore and aft containing the crew, instrumentation and possibly also the fuel, and a rear section carrying the tail unit and a propulsion unit with a pusher propeller.' Furthermore, the aircraft was to be protected by 'an outer skin having increased resistance against bullets in the usual manner, for example, by several millimetres of strong steel plating.' Dornier saw the main advantage to this layout as being the increased power of a two-engined design without the attendant drag issues of two engine nacelles. Thus it was that Professor Dornier began to design an aircraft that would incorporate these features, resulting in the Dornier Do P.59 of November 1937.

To assist in assessing the practical application of his concept, Dornier brought in Austrian Dr.-Ing. Ulrich Hütter. A graduate in Mechanical Engineering and Shipbuilding Studies from the *Technische Hochschule* in Vienna, Hütter subsequently went on to study aeronautical engineering at the *Technische Hochschule* in Stuttgart, from where he obtained a diploma. He designed a seaplane, the H 28, with his brother Wolfgang, before joining Schempp-Hirth, a glider and aircraft parts

Mechanics give the diminutive Göppingen Gö 9 a sense of scale as they manhandle the aircraft over the concrete. The four-bladed rear propeller was fixed to a drive shaft that ran through the cruciform tail section. A small tailwheel can be seen at the tip of the lower fin.

The highly experienced Dornier test-pilot Flugkapitän Hermann 'Iwan' Quenzler stands up in the cockpit of the Gö 9 during flight testing in June 1941. Seen in this photograph are the vents for the 80hp Hirth I M60 R air-cooled in-line engine just aft of the cockpit. Quenzler would go on to fly a number of the Do 335 prototypes.

company formed by Martin Schempp with the help of Wolf Hirth, the one-legged gliding pioneer, where Hütter worked on the design and construction of dive-brake systems and gliders. He also became involved in the science of aircraft construction, aircraft static and fluid mechanics, flight mechanics, advanced mathematics, machine elements and kinematics.

Dornier commissioned Hütter to build a small aircraft to serve as a test-bed for his push-pull design, and the result was the Göppingen Gö 9, so named after the town in southern Germany close to where Schempp-Hirth was based. The Gö 9, registered D-EBYW, had a cylindrical fuselage, at the end of which was a cruciform tail unit. The lower fin of the latter was fitted with a small wheel intended to prevent the rear propeller from striking the ground on takeoff. In plan and frontal view at least, it was effectively a 1:2.5 scale model of the Do 17Z. The aircraft was 6.8m in length and had a span of 7.2m. It weighed 720kg. The cockpit, located well forward, had an all-round vision canopy, beneath which was a nose wheel that was part of a fully retractable tricycle landing gear.

The aircraft was powered by an 80hp Hirth I M60 R air-cooled in-line engine that was installed just aft of the cockpit, in the centre of the fuselage and above the wings, which, likewise, were mounted mid-fuselage. A shaft ran the length of the rear fuselage and drove the four-bladed, wooden pusher propeller.

The Gö 9 underwent extensive testing on the ground, frequently without its canopy fitted, and with the propeller both static and running, before the first flight trials took place in June 1941. For these, the aircraft was flown by Dornier test-pilot Hermann 'Iwan' Quenzler after it had been towed into the air by Do 17M CO+JB. In later tests, all funded by Dornier, the Gö 9 was able to take off under its own power and achieved a maximum speed of 220km/h.

Quenzler was an eminently qualified aviator, having joined Dornier in January 1936, and he would test-fly the Do 18, Do 24 and Do 26 flying boats, as well as the Do 17 bomber. He reported that the Gö 9 handled well, and that the rear engine and pusher propeller functioned without problem.

At one stage, the aircraft was earmarked by the RLM for testing other tricycle undercarriages, but it was eventually dismantled at Weilheim an der Teck in 1945 after it was found to be too heavy following the fitment of additional equipment intended for such testing. The Gö 9 met its end when it was set alight by liberated slave-workers.

What was gleaned from tests with the Gö 9 aided Dornier in the honing of his plans for the Do P.59 project, to which he assigned a pair of 1,000hp DB 601 engines. As the project drawings were refined, so a radiator intake was added for the forward, nose-mounted powerplant, while intakes for the mid-mounted rear engine were positioned on either side of the fuselage. Like the Gö 9, the P.59 had a cruciform tail, but the lower fin was fitted with a skid rather than a wheel. Dornier foresaw an aircraft 11.36m in length with a span of 11m and a landing weight of 4,500kg. It was calculated that the P.59 would carry a fuel load of 650 litres and have a maximum speed of 595km/h (sea level) and 715km/h (altitude).

The P.59 languished, largely forgotten, until late 1942 when the RLM revisited the concept of back-to-back engine propulsion for a high-speed fighter-bomber able to carry 500kg of bombs at 750km/h over a range of up to 2,000km. Undaunted by the competing proposals from Arado, Junkers and Messerschmitt, Dornier returned to the P.59, and on 4 January 1943 he submitted two versions of a project known as the P.231, *Entwurf* 1 and 2. From early December, much of the work had been undertaken by *Ing.* Werner Fleck who, having joined the design team in 1938, had worked on the development of the Do 24 and Do 26 flying boats.

In both cases, the overall design of the P.231 was similar to the P.59, but with the addition of a tricycle undercarriage. However, in *Entwurf* 2, Dornier adopted the radical proposal of mating two fuselages using a common wing centre section, similar in appearance to the Bf 109Z. The aircraft was to be powered by two nose-mounted engines, but it was soon realized that *Entwurf* 1 was lighter and thus 40km/h faster than its fellow variant, with a maximum speed of 840km/h. The *Entwurf* 2 proposal was dropped and the focus switched to three sub-variants of the single-fuselage project.

The P.231/1, which omitted the variable incidence wing intended for the P.59m, was powered by two 1,800hp DB 603E engines and had a wingspan of 15m. Measuring 12.9m in length, the project was to remain unarmed, presumably to ensure speed, but it was to carry an internal ordnance load of 500kg. With a length of 13.25m, the P.231/2

Holding what could be a piece of the Gö 9's control surfaces that has come loose, a mechanic runs alongside the aircraft as it undertakes a ground test under tow. Flugkapitän Quenzler is visible in the cockpit.

was similar in composition, but it was fitted with a pair of 1,900hp DB 603GM engines and featured lower aspect ratio wings with a span of 13.2m. The P.231/3 was effectively the same, but the rear piston engine was to be replaced by an unspecified turbojet unit.

The four firms competing for the twin-engined *Schnellbomber* design submitted their proposals at a meeting of the RLM on 19 January 1943. By this time, opinion seems to have shifted from the somewhat sceptical position held by the Ministry the previous year, and Dornier was fortunate to have impressed no less a figure than the *Generalluftzeugmeister* himself, Generalfeldmarschall Erhard Milch.

In the first week of the new year, Professor Dornier had visited the hard-headed Milch and shown him drawings of an aircraft which, with its unusual, fuselage-mounted, double-engined arrangement, initially Milch found perplexing. He was aware that Oberstleutnant Ulrich Diesing, head of the RLM's *Technischen Luftrüstung* (Technical Equipment), had already rejected the quirky design, but Milch respected Dornier and took a closer look at his proposal. After some consideration, he concluded that Dornier's project could fly in excess of 750km/h. He told the aircraft designer, unofficially, that he would place an order for 20 such aircraft.

A few days later, Dornier's submission was given approval. He was authorized to proceed with the production of ten prototypes, one of which was to be a machine deliberately assigned for testing to destruction. The RLM's decision had probably been influenced by the fact that there was still no certainty over delivery of the much-vaunted jet engines then under development, and so piston-engined fighters and bombers would continue to be manufactured. That being said, speed was the essential criteria, and if a design could be realized that incorporated two engines in one fuselage, thus reducing drag but increasing speed, as well as consuming standard fuel, all well and good.

Official orders were issued by the RLM on 27 January, but the requirement had widened. This was to be a truly multi-role aircraft able to operate as an interceptor, fast bomber and reconnaissance machine.

CHAPTER THREE

'A REVOLUTIONARY INNOVATION'

The gestation of what would become the Do 335 was characterized by a process of design reviews. Even as the first prototype – the V1 – was under construction at Manzell and Meersburg on the shores of the Bodensee, the Dornier firm instigated changes to the appearance of the aircraft. Various models were made that were intended to inform the design and engineering team on stability. These models underwent extensive testing, initially in a wind tunnel, during which one of them was hung, then dropped into a flow of wind while a film was made of the effects. The model was painted black with white lines so that assessment measurements could be made more easily. In another test, a compressed air catapult system 'fired' a model of the planned Do 335 across a runway several times in different directions in order for it to 'land' on its tricycle undercarriage, which it did successfully. In a further trial, a model was launched in a similar fashion over the waters of the Bodensee, measurements being taken until it came to a stop on the surface.

As a result of these tests, the design of the Do 335 was broadly similar to the P.231/2, but with an annular radiator added to the underside of the fuselage for the forward engine and a large scoop intake incorporated in the rear fuselage for the aft engine. The design also featured undercarriage doors that slid downwards to cover the housings in the wings as the wheels retracted.

Both engines of the Do 335 V1 are run up at Mengen, producing what must have been a deafening noise.

The first prototype Do 335, V1 Wk-Nr 230001 CP+UA, at Mengen in the autumn of 1943. There appears to be some damage visible on the engine access panel, as well as exhaust staining.

Resting somewhat precariously in a wooden cradle, Do 335 V1 Wk-Nr 230001 CP+UA is transported on the back of a trailer towed by a tractor from Manzell to Mengen, some 50km away. Visible here is the tip of the rear of the drive shaft for the aft engine propeller and the rear DB 603A itself, exposed because of the removal of the access panel.

A mock-up of the aircraft was inspected by RLM officials on 18 April 1943, followed by testing of the rear engine fitment on 27 August. No problems were experienced and the RLM was sufficiently satisfied by this stage to order a further ten prototypes, taking the total order to 20 aircraft.

Following completion of the fuselage and wing section of the Do 335 V1, Wk-Nr 230001 CP+UA, the components were made ready for relocation by road 50km north, to Mengen, where they would be assembled and the completed aircraft would undertake flight trials. However, a complication ensued when it was discovered that the fuselage was too large to get out of its assembly shed at Manzell, and so the building had to be dismantled! The fuselage was then loaded onto an open, four-wheeled trailer and towed by a small tractor along the country roads to Mengen.

After assembly, and powered by two DB 603A engines that were checked thoroughly before take-off, the V1 made its first flight from the Dornier works at Friedrichshafen. The DB 603 was a development of the DB 601/605 series of 12-cylinder, liquid-cooled, inverted vee, in-line engines, and it was the only powerplant to be fitted to the Do 335. Each unit had a capacity of 44.5 litres and gave 1,750hp at 2,700rpm. One engine weighed 910kg, and it was 2.610m in length, 0.830m wide and 1.156m high.

DORNIER Do 335 INSTRUMENT PANEL

1. Throttle levers
2. Trim indicator
3. Propeller selector, landing flap and undercarriage switches
4. Undercarriage position indicators
5. Gyro control switch
6. External air temperature indicator
7. Radio altimeter
8. Clock
9. Altimeter
10. Airspeed indicator
11. Oxygen pressure gauge
12. Main electrics emergency switch
13. Master compass
14. Artificial horizon
15. Revi 16D gunsight
16. Variometer
17. Radio navigation indicator
18. Propeller pitch indicators
19. Combined pressure/RPM indicators
20. Coolant and oil temperature and fuel and oil pressure gauges
21. Left horn of control column = bomb release. Right horn = fuselage cannon firing button. The button for the MG 151 was on the forward face of the horn
22. Fire warning lamps
23. Gauges for ejector seat system compressed air pressure; emergency compressed air pressure; oil pressure
24. FuG 16Z(Y) control panel

The size of the Do 335 is illustrated well in this photograph of the V1. Note how a man of average height could walk easily under the aircraft without needing to crouch to any great extent. The front propeller spinner is not fitted in this view of preparations for an engine test.

The V1 was flown by Flugkapitän Hans Dieterle, who was renowned for having secured the world speed record for Germany while flying the Heinkel He 100 experimental fighter, in which he reached a speed of 746.606km/h while flying between Oranienburg and Neuruppin on 30 March 1939.

Born on 29 June 1915 in Rottweil in southern Germany, Hans Dieterle had joined Heinkel as a test pilot in 1937. He had subsequently attempted several record flights, including the world 1,000km closed-circuit speed record in the He 119 V4 while flying with Gerhard Nitschke as his co-pilot. On one such speed flight, however, the Heinkel crashed and Nitschke was killed, although Dieterle escaped injured. The speed he achieved in his record flight in the He 100 V8 was surpassed just a month after he had made it, when Messerschmitt test-pilot Fritz Wendel succeeded in flying even faster in the Me 209 V4. Dieterle left Heinkel on 1 September 1941 to join Dornier as the company's chief test pilot.

Heinkel test pilot Hans Dieterle smiles from the cockpit of the record-breaking He 100 V8, in which he achieved the world record for speed on 30 March 1939 for attaining 746.606km/h. Dieterle would later join Dornier and be a key figure in the Do 335 test programme. Indeed, he was at the controls of the first prototype on its inaugural flight.

The cockpit of Do 335 V3 Wk-Nr 230003 CP+UC. To the pilot's left is the console for the throttle levers, whilst in the centre is the main instrument panel, which includes an airspeed indicator, artificial horizon, compass and radio navigation indicator. The levers on either side of the cockpit edge are to effect jettison of the canopy. To the far left of the photograph can be seen the edge of the pilot's headrest as well as the raised armrest.

After climbing up a step ladder, Dieterle settled into the Do 335's roomy cockpit. Directly ahead of him on the instrument panel were the six main instruments comprising airspeed indicator, artificial horizon, variometer, altimeter, compass and radio navigation indicator. To the left of this group were the clock, radio altimeter and ambient temperature gauge. To the right of these dials were the propeller pitch indicators, below which were the rpm and oil temperature and pressure gauges. Reaching to the left, the pilot had easy access to the throttles, while to the right was the box containing the Lorenz FuG 16Z(Y) VHF R/T. On either side of the pilot, mounted on the rim of the cockpit, were two large canopy jettison levers. Above the main instrument panel was the reflector gunsight.

Dieterle took the Do 335 V1 aloft for the first time on 26 October 1943, the flight being watched by Claude Dornier and Luftwaffe observers from the ground. Things went reasonably well, the only cause for any alarm being that the main wheels failed to lock in place. After landing it was discovered that a design fault meant that the wheel well covers prevented full retraction. This was rectified by the removal of the covers – something that became a permanent feature of this machine. Dieterle flew the V1 again on 29 and 30 October, but difficulties with the undercarriage lingered.

Dornier's other test pilots, Flieger-Hauptingenieur Werner Altrogge and Hermann Quenzler, soon joined the flight-test programme, with Altrogge flying the V1 on 2 November 1943.

An extremely experienced airman, Altrogge was born on 3 December 1913 in Obernkirchen. He qualified with his Dipl.-Ing. from the *Technische Hochschule* in Hannover in May 1937 and joined the

Considerable activity surrounds Do 335 V1 CP+UA at Mengen on 26 October 1943. The upper gull wing engine panels are open, as is the underside access panel, while the open cockpit canopy is hinged to the right. Note that although the aircraft's undercarriage is fully extended, its wheels are off the ground as the weight of the Do 335 is supported by wooden trestles. The step ladder indicates the considerable height from the ground of the cockpit – more like that of a bomber.

Erprobungsstelle at Rechlin on 15 July of that year, from where he made numerous flights to test Focke-Wulf, Flettner and Focke-Achgelis helicopters and autogyros. Altrogge was later assigned to operational postings with the Luftwaffe, including service with 9./LG 2 in early 1940, then 3.(F)/Od.d.L., with whom he flew high-altitude reconnaissance missions in the Ju 86R over Britain and Russia. He was promoted to Flieger-Hauptingenieur on 23 February 1942 and received the *Frontflugspange für Aufklärer* (Operational Flying Clasp for Reconnaissance Flyers). Altrogge joined Dornier just over a year later on 22 March 1943.

During November and December 1943, a programme of 23 test-flights was made in the V1 by Dieterle, Altrogge and Quenzler. These were intended to assess general flight and handling characteristics, including longitudinal stability, diving, rudder control, nose gear, ailerons, trim tabs and undercarriage, as well as pressure testing for the flaps. A number of the test flights were filmed both on the ground and in the air. Climbing and speed tests were also flown, with Altrogge reaching 600km/h at sea level on 5 November, during which speed measurements and stopping distances were evaluated.

A single-engined flight was attempted on the 15th, which revealed that the Do 335 could fly faster with its forward engine stopped than with the rear propeller feathered. With the forward motor stopped, a speed of 560km/h was achievable in level flight. Furthermore, when flying on one engine, none of the asymmetric problems experienced with conventional twin-engined aircraft came into play.

On 19 December, Hermann Quenzler tested the wing characteristics following the adoption of a new, sharper leading edge profile, the air flow being assessed by photographing the effect on wool tufts fitted to the area. He also tested the aileron controls to check operation of the

ball bearings in the wings, as well as stability of the ailerons. All were good. On the 20th, Altrogge even flew a simulated combat encounter with a Do 217 bomber.

One problem, however, was that the rear Daimler-Benz tended to overheat as a result of inadequate cooling, and this was to prove a perpetual problem throughout the type's life. A series of ground tests failed to solve this, as well as the ongoing undercarriage issues.

On 23 December, the RLM's assigned *Typenbegleiter* (type coordinator), Fliegerstabsing Voigt, also flew the V1 in a series of short flights that extended into January in order to assess general flight-handling. Again, all seems to have been in order.

On 31 December, the second prototype, V2 Wk-Nr. 230002 CP+UB, joined the test programme, being flown the same day by Hans Dieterle. Fitted with DB 603A-2 12-cylinder, inverted vee, liquid-cooled, in-line engines of 1,750hp, with direct fuel injection and a single-stage, hydraulically driven supercharger, the V2 was different to its earlier sister aircraft in a number of ways. The principle change was the redesigned forward cowling that now accommodated the oil cooler intake – something Dornier had decided to do following the wind tunnel tests. This adjustment had proven more satisfactory than the Messerschmitt-originated Daimler-Benz design. The V2 also had modified main wheel doors, which were fixed to the undercarriage legs, and the cockpit canopy was now hinged to the rear, replacing the sliding type fitted to the V1.

Similar flight tests to the V1 were undertaken by the V2, but if anything they were more rigorous and investigated horizontal and climbing flight, single-engine flying, undercarriage functioning and trouble-shooting associated with the cooling system for the rear engine. The canopy of this machine was completed with a blister on both sides, into each of which was fitted a mirror to aid rearward visibility.

The forward Daimler-Benz DB 603 engine is run up during a test. The pilot to the right, his hands covering his ears, lends scale to the nosewheel and mainwheels. The item of equipment suspended from the open nosewheel bay was trailed behind the aircraft during flight to measure pressure during speed and altitude tests.

With its weight being taken by two slender-looking jacks, one of the most advanced piston-engined aircraft of World War II undergoes undercarriage retraction tests in front of a rudimentary shelter for one of the oldest forms of mechanical transport – bicycles!

The V3, Wk-Nr 230003 CP+UC, was in general terms a similar aircraft to the V2, but differed principally in being powered by two DB 603G-0 engines rated at 2,000hp. It featured improved exhausts and wing root fairings, and also the blistered canopy. The latter was constructed of 11 Plexiglas panels that hinged to the right to open, and when closed, rested on a fixed windscreen made up of five curved panels. Just forward of each blister was a small, hinged clear-vision panel. It also had a fold-down access ladder that was lowered from a small bay in the underside of the left wing root.

The V3 was flown for the first time on 20 January 1944 by Altrogge, but further testing was delayed when the nosewheel broke during landing at Mengen – the result of poor welding of the retraction cylinder. By this stage of the war, deterioration in manufacturing standards, and inferior components, was becoming a problem – and not just with Dornier aircraft. Nevertheless, it is fair to say that the sheer weight of the Do 335 placed a commensurately heavy load on the gear legs, and a lack of hydraulic pressure would result in the undercarriage being pushed up into the wing when heavy landings were made. Comparatively, for a fighter, the main wheels were very large, measuring 1,015mm x 380mm, while the nosewheel tyre was 685mm x 250mm.

Despite such problems, the aircraft was making an impression with the RLM, and on 10 January 1944, following a decree by Generalfeldmarschall Milch, the roles foreseen for the Do 335 were prioritized as high-speed bomber, 'heavy' fighter, nightfighter and reconnaissance machine. Indeed, with RAF Bomber Command's nocturnal campaign against the cities, factories and transport infrastructure of the Third Reich showing no sign of abating, on 20 January, a new order for a further ten prototypes was issued exclusively for nightfighter development. Milch had favoured the Do 335 for

several weeks by this time, believing it to be the high-speed, piston-engined fighter and bomber of the future, and one that would be more than able to hold its own against aircraft such as the American P-38 Lightning. But, as ever in the technical and military history of the Third Reich, Milch had had to tread carefully.

In September 1943, Professor Willy Messerschmitt, eager to promote his new jet engine-powered Me 262 interceptor, had visited Hitler, and in the course of his meeting he attempted to persuade the *Führer* to cancel production of the rival Do 335 in order to release manufacturing capacity for the Me 262. In this he failed – for the time being. But aside from Messerschmitt, Albert Speer, the Minister for Armaments who held favour with Hitler, believed that the resources being expended on the Dornier project would be better used for increased army production.

By mid-January 1944, several senior Luftwaffe officers had flown the Do 335, including Generalmajor Dietrich Peltz, the *General der Kampfflieger* (General of Bombers), Oberstleutnant Ulrich Diesing (see Chapter Two) and Oberst Edgar Petersen, the *Kommandeur der Erprobungsstellen* (Commander of Luftwaffe Test Centres). Collectively, at a meeting in Milch's office on 14 January, these officers opined that the Dornier's flight-handling and stability were acceptable, as were the new company-designed cowlings (which were viewed as being far superior to the original Messerschmitt ones), although there was room for improvement in other areas.

In terms of production, the RLM envisaged 82 Do 335s being completed by the end of 1944, although the fighter version would be delayed. Construction of the first pre-production model – the Do 335A-0 – was expected to commence in August 1944 with a run of 270 machines at the Dornier Süd works in Munich, and at Oberpfaffenhofen and Friedrichshafen. The Friedrichshafen plant

The fuselage of Do 335A-0 Wk-Nr 240110 VG+PP under construction at a sawmill at Ummendorf, which was one of several dispersed sites used for stages of assembly in the Oberpfaffenhofen and Friedrichshafen areas. Clearly visible are the paste-filled panel lines, the wing root and fairing for the under-fuselage radiator scoop.

A Do 335 ejection seat taken from an aircraft captured by the Allies. The seat was built with a headrest, liftable armrests and foot supports.

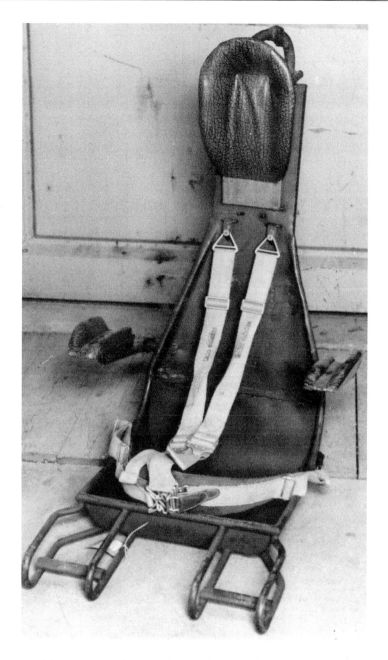

would oversee production from sub-assembly plants at Manzell, Löwental, Allmansweier, Ringbauhalle, Wangen, Langenargen, Rickenbach, Dornbirn, Bregenz, Pfronten, Mengen and a number of dispersed sites, from all of which 77,800m² would be assigned to production of the Do 335. The Munich plant would oversee the Neuenberg, Augsburg-Ost, Oberpfaffenhofen, Neuhausen, Landsberg and other dispersed sites, from all of which 87,100m² would be used for production. An example of one of the dispersed sites was a sawmill at Ummendorf, between Friedrichshafen and Ulm, where fuselage sections for the A-0 were to be completed prior to final assembly some

170km to the east at Oberpfaffenhofen. The master production plan, *Lieferplan* 225/1 of 13 January 1944, stated that Friedrichshafen was to turn out 120 pre-production aircraft by March 1946.

The A-0 and the A-1 series production variants were planned as *Schnellbombers* powered by DB 603A-2 engines (later DB 603E). With ordnance suspended from the *Schloss* series of bomb racks fitted into an internal bay beneath the main fuel tank, these variants were able to carry mixed configurations ranging from 8 x SC 50 (i.e., 50kg) or SD 70 fragmentation bombs, 2 x SC 250 or 500kg bombs or various types of bomb containers of the same weight. Armament was provided in the form of two 20mm MG 151/20 cannon mounted above the engine and a 30mm MK 103 cannon in a Motorkanone installation, firing through the hollow propeller hub. The pilot would aim these weapons via a Revi 16D reflex sight.

Radio and communications equipment comprised a FuG 16Z R/T-receiver, a FuG 25a IFF (Identification, Friend or Foe) set and a FuG 125 VHF radio beacon signal receiver.

A strengthened B-series *Zerstörer* (destroyer or heavy fighter) was planned for commencement in February 1945, which Milch saw as providing a replacement for the ageing Bf 110 and as a more sophisticated aircraft than the Me 410 – it would be distinguished externally from the A-series by a vee-shaped armoured windscreen. These B-1 and B-2 sub-types were to be manufactured by Dornier in Munich.

When the Luftwaffe first received the Do 335, it is easy to understand the astonishment of its personnel at the sheer size of the colossal aircraft. A man of average height could walk beneath any part of it with ease. The forward engine was mounted on a pair of welded pressed steel box section bearers attached by self-aligning bolts to four steel fittings on the front bulkhead. The engine cowling was formed of two sections fastened by toggles to the exhaust manifolds. The radiators for lubricant and coolant were annular in shape and located around the engine nose casting, the airflow being controlled by a ring of hydraulically operated gills. The propeller was a three-bladed VDM, 3.5m in diameter.

The pilot was accommodated directly behind the ammunition containers. He was encased by a rearwards-hinging canopy, the windscreen of which had two electrically heated glazed panels. The blisters first trialled in the V3 became standard and held a small mirror for rearward vision. A Heinkel-designed armoured ejection seat was operated by compressed air from bottles carried in the nose wheel compartment. A 15mm-thick armour plate was built in behind the pilot, and aft of this were the two 45-litre lubricating oil tanks, one on the left for the forward engine and one on the right side for the rear. Between these could be mounted three pressurized tanks for the GM 1 nitrous-oxide power-boosting system. The space below housed the nose gear when retracted. Aft of this was positioned the main 1,230-litre self-sealing fuel tank, with the bomb-bay beneath. This had two hinged doors and could house a 500kg bomb that would be winched up into the bay using an intricate hoisting system. Alternative

OPPOSITE
A schematic from May 1944 showing the control system, hydraulics and compressed air canisters for the ejection seat as fitted to the Do 335 V8.

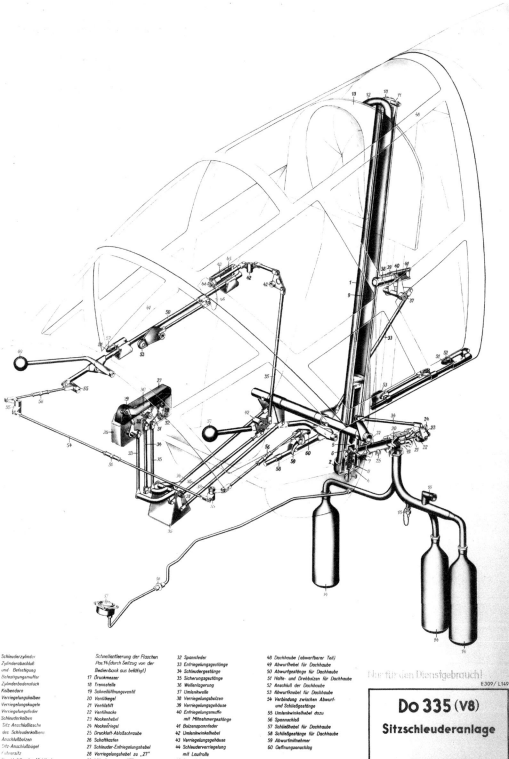

1 Schleuderzylinder
2 Zylinderabschluß
   und Befestigung
3 Befestigungsmutter
4 Zylinderbodenstück
5 Kolbendorn
6 Verriegelungskolben
7 Verriegelungskugeln
8 Verriegelungsfeder
9 Schleuderkolben
10 Sitz Anschlußflasche
   des Schleuderkolbens
11 Anschußbolzen
12 Sitz-Anschlußbügel
13 Führersitz
14 Druckluftflasche (2 Liter)
15 Druckluft-Füllventil
16 Anschluß für Ventil zur

Schnellentleerung der Flaschen
Pos.14 (durch Seilzug von der
Bedienbank aus betätigt)
17 Druckmesser
18 Trennstelle
19 Schnellöffnungsventil
20 Ventilkegel
21 Ventilstift
22 Ventilnocke
23 Nockenhebel
24 Nockenriegel
25 Druckluft-Ablaßschraube
26 Schaltkasten
27 Schleuder-Entriegelungshebel
28 Verriegelungshebel zu „27"
29 Mitnehmer zu „27"
30 Schleuderhebel
31 Schleuderzwischenhebel

32 Spannfeder
33 Entriegelungsgestänge
34 Schleudergestänge
35 Sicherungsgestänge
36 Wellenlagerung
37 Umlenkwelle
38 Verriegelungsbolzen
39 Verriegelungsgehäuse
40 Entriegelungsmuffe
   mit Mitnehmergestänge
41 Bolzenspannfeder
42 Umlenkwinkelhebel
43 Verriegelungsgehäuse
44 Schleuderverriegelung
   mit Laufrolle
45 Spannfeder dazu
46 Verriegelungsschild
47 Dachhaube (fester Teil)

48 Dachhaube (abwerfbarer Teil)
49 Abwurfhebel für Dachhaube
50 Abwurfgestänge für Dachhaube
51 Halte- und Drehbolzen für Dachhaube
52 Anschluß der Dachhaube
53 Abwurfknebel für Dachhaube
54 Verbindung zwischen Abwurf-
   und Schließgestänge
55 Umlenkwinkelhebel dazu
56 Spannschloß
57 Schließhebel für Dachhaube
58 Schließgestänge für Dachhaube
59 Abwurfmitnehmer
60 Oeffnungsanschlag

Nur für den Dienstgebrauch!

E309/L149

Do 335 (V8)

Sitzschleuderanlage

Stand vom Mai 1944

Inzwischen eingetretene Änderungen beachten u.
darauf hinweisen.

sub-type configurations allowed for a jettisonable 500-litre auxiliary fuel tank, or for the carrying of ordnance of double the weight, or for the carriage of one or two Rb 50/30 cameras and/or a 250-litre auxiliary tank for GM 1.

Behind this was the rear DB 603 QA engine, which was mounted on four steel brackets bolted to steel fittings on the fuselage longerons. The 'Q' sub-designation indicated that the engine had been adapted to perform with opposite rotation to that of a standard engine. The 3.30m diameter VDM propeller aft of the cruciform tail was driven from the reduction gear at the back of the engine through a 115mm diameter tubular steel shaft, 1.60m long with a splined sleeve at each end. The shaft extended beyond the tail. The rear engine shaft was to prove problematic during testing and operations with the Do 335, mainly because it was not strong or large enough to deal with the forces expected of it.

A coolant tank was mounted above the engine, while below and behind was positioned the radiator, fed by a large under-fuselage scoop. The air flow through the coolant radiator was controlled by a pair of hydraulically operated doors just above the rudder, and that through the lubricant radiator by another hydraulically operated door just forward of the lower fin. The exhausts projected through holes in the side doors of the engine compartment.

Also in this compartment were the oil cooler, fire extinguisher and radio equipment. The latter comprised the Lorenz FuG 16 ZY transceiver, which was used for communications and fighter control, the GEMA FuG 25 a *Erstling* IFF set, which worked with the *Freya, Würzburg* and *Gemse* ground radars, and the Lorenz FuG 125 *Hermine* radio beacon. The aerial for the FuG 16 was mounted inside the dorsal fin while the FuG 25 employed a ring antenna above the fuselage centre section.

The fuselage tank access panel was in the top of the fuselage, as were the rear engine doors, while the underside held the housings for the nose wheel doors, the bomb-bay doors and the radiator ducts. This meant that the sides of the fuselage, together with a number of heavy

Do 335 V8 Wk-Nr 230008 CP+UH was probably photographed at Löwental in the summer of 1944. The aircraft undertook a range of test flights at Rechlin, but was troubled by undercarriage problems.

longerons, formed a pair of plate web girders with strength to resist the longitudinal bending imposed by the vertical tail loads and the weights of the two engines, the fuselage tanks and the bomb racks. The sides were braced together to resist bending imposed by lateral loads by the floor of the cabin and tank bay and by a vee bracing of tubes below the rear engine. Like the problems with the rear engine shaft, the fuselage behind the rear engine was weak and of insufficient strength to be a part of the load-bearing structure, resulting in occasional cracking.

Armament for the Do 335 took the form of two 20mm MG 151/20 cannon mounted above the engine and synchronized to fire through the propeller arc. Ammunition was stored in two containers located by the cannon, each of 200 rounds capacity. A single, long-barrelled Rheinmetall 30mm MK 103 cannon, a weapon that had a greater muzzle velocity than the 30mm MK 108 cannon, was mounted between the engine cylinder banks and fired through the spinner. Ammunition was fed from a 70-round container mounted behind and below the weapon. The first prototype to be fitted with armament was Do 335 V5 CP+UE, which made its inaugural flight in February 1944, but would not undergo significant testing until August.

The wings were constructed around a single box spar with all-metal stressed skinning. Trapezoidal in planform, they had a 13-degree sweepback on the leading edge and a six-degree sweep forward on the trailing edge. The wings were removable at the root and were based on a single rectangular box section spar, with its centre 33 per cent of the chord from the leading edge at the root. The spar was of Duralumin construction with steel root fittings. At the root it was 570mm wide by 535mm deep, and tapered gradually towards the wing tips, which were blunt. The Duralumin skin covering was 1.5mm thick. The inner section of the wing leading edge, extending approximately 1,000mm from the root, was of a sharp nose section designed to control the propeller wash over the tailplane to improve low-speed manoeuvrability and to diffuse stall characteristics by minimizing buffeting. De-icing of the wing leading edges was provided.

A series of compressed air bottles was carried in the centre of the wing root section to lower the undercarriage in case of hydraulic failure. A 310-litre self-sealing fuel tank was mounted in the leading edge of each wing. In the Do 335B-series, this tank was replaced by containers for the 70 rounds of 30mm MK 103 ammunition that were protected from the front by a rectangular armour plate. New, square fuel tanks of similar capacity to those for the A-series were mounted in the outboard portion of the wing. The wing root was enclosed by a fairing secured by a cable passing through hooks on the fuselage. Variable camber all-metal flaps were positioned inboard of the ailerons. Each flap had a metal skin of 0.5mm thickness attached to plate ribs at 200mm pitch. The spar, which was placed 25 per cent of the chord from the leading edge, was a plate 1mm thick, with its edges turned over and riveted to the skin. The flap was mounted on three hinges on brackets attached to the wing ribs and was actuated by a hydraulic jack located inside the wing.

The hydraulically powered ailerons were of similar construction to the flaps and were mounted on three brackets. They were operated by a

A new DB 603 engine is winched along a gantry for fitting into a Do 335 at Oberpfaffenhofen.

system of 40mm diameter Duralumin push-pull tubes and bell cranks. An additional link connected with the flap was introduced so that the ailerons were dropped when the flaps were lowered. The metal trim tab was operated by a system of shafts and universal joints from the lateral trim control in the cockpit.

The cruciform tail was also built of metal, with the exception of the leading edge of the dorsal fin, which was made of wood and housed the FuG 16 ZY radio aerial. Each tailplane was of two spar construction and was covered by three 0.9mm-thick stressed skin panels, as was the 'D' section leading edge and the upper and lower panels between the spars. The inside was accessible before the root and tip ribs were fitted. The tip was separate, being attached with screws to the tip rib. The inboard end of each spar carried steel fittings for two bolts, by which it was attached to the fuselage. Slotted forward attachment bolts enabled tailplane incidence to be adjusted on the ground. De-icing was provided to the leading edges of the tailplane.

The dorsal and ventral fins were of similar construction to the tailplane, apart from the wooden leading edge of the upper unit. The tip of the lower fin was strengthened and hinged to the bottom of an oleo strut located inside the fin that was designed to act as a safety skid. This complete ventral fin could be jettisoned in the event of a belly landing.

Rudders and elevators were both aerodynamically and mass-balanced. The former had a single spar consisting of a plate with edges flanged and riveted to the skin placed at 20 per cent of the chord from the leading edge. Plate ribs with dished lightening holes were spaced at 150mm pitch and the metal skin was 0.5mm thick. The elevators were of similar construction to the rudders. The dorsal and ventral rudders and both elevators could not be directly connected because of the rear propeller drive shaft. Instead, they were linked to welded steel cranks on counter shafts controlled from the cockpit via a 32mm diameter push-pull Duralumin tube.

Each of the main wheels was mounted on a single oleo-pneumatic leg with torque links, and they retracted inwards into the wing. Retraction

The rear DB 603 engine shortly after being fitted into place in the fuselage of Do 335A-0 Wk-Nr 240110 at Ummendorf. Note to the right that the engine unit has not yet been connected to the rear propeller drive shaft.

was carried out by two hydraulic cylinders. The main one was a double-acting cylinder alongside the oleo strut, its lower end attached to the short arm of a bell crank mounted on the oleo strut. Its longer arm carried a pair of rollers that engaged with a pair of cam plates attached to the lower components of the twin side stays. The auxiliary single-acting cylinder, placed horizontally inside the wing, was connected with the oleo strut by a cable passing over a multiplying pulley that doubled the effective travel of the jack.

On reaching its fully retracted position, the oleo strut 'tipped up' a 'U'-shaped member that embraced the strut and was secured by a mechanical spring latch. This latch could be released by a small hydraulic cylinder connected in parallel with the extended side of the main jack or by a cable leading to a handle on the instrument panel. When pressure was applied to the extending line, the up lock was released and the main cylinder lowered the undercarriage, the cable pulling the auxiliary plunger back into its cylinder.

The main wheel undercarriage doors were attached to the oleo-pneumatic leg, but auxiliary doors were fitted to the wheel well on the underside of the wing. This door, which covered the lower half of the wheel, was normally held open by a spring but was closed by a bar, against which the tyre hit during the last stage of its upward travel.

The nose wheel was mounted in a welded steel fork at the lower end of a single oleo-pneumatic strut and folded backwards into a housing beneath the pilot's seat. The wheel well was covered by side doors linked to the strut, and they were closed when the strut was fully retracted. The wheel fork was provided with a hydraulic shimmy damper and a spring plunger centring device.

The brakes differed from normal German practice in that they were operated by the engine pump. The master cylinders, which were usually actuated by tilting the rudder pedals, were replaced by control valves that allowed differing pressure to be applied to each main wheel brake independently.

Delivery of prototypes continued to trickle through during the spring of 1944, with Do 335 V6 Wk-Nr 230006 CP+UF being the fifth example to fly, with Altrogge at the controls, on 25 March. This aircraft was used primarily for testing various equipment such as hydraulics, emergency systems, undercarriage and also the FuG 101 radio altimeter.

But there was a major blow to the programme on 15 April 1944. The second prototype, airborne from Mengen with Werner Altrogge at the controls in order to evaluate roll characteristics, began to run low on fuel. The pilot altered his course for an interim landing at Leipheim but, shortly after he did so, the aircraft's rear engine caught fire. When Altrogge attempted to activate the fire extinguisher system it failed. With no other option, he decided to bail out using the ejector seat. However, as he unlocked the canopy, rather than it falling away behind the aircraft, it came down on the pilot's head, fracturing his skull. With Altrogge unconscious, the Do 335 V2 veered off course and dived vertically into the ground at Buxheim, near Memmingen, missing a nursery school by just 50m. Altrogge was killed. It is believed that the fire had been caused by hot gases escaping as a result of a spark plug popping out from the engine block, which then burned into a fuel line which, in turn, set the whole engine area alight.

Another blow came a few days later when, on the 24th, the V6 was badly damaged during a USAAF bombing raid on Friedrichshafen-Löwental. It was decided to deploy what remained of the aircraft for ground tests, with the fuselage being moved to the Junkers engine plant at Dessau. Here, it was used to test rear engine temperatures in simulated flight, with a large fan being placed immediately in front of the fuselage – which was resting in a cradle – to replicate airflow. One somewhat crude and drastic method employed for these tests was to

In this photograph, a DB 603 has been installed and fitted to the rear propeller drive shaft. This engine would have been modified so that its rotation was the opposite to a standard forward unit.

inject fuel along pipework running beneath the engine cowling, the vapour from which was then ignited. The resulting temperature was duly noted and compared with that used to activate the fire warning system in the cockpit. Remarkably, the V6 fuselage survived several such tests before it eventually succumbed to fire.

Meanwhile, following the loss of Werner Altrogge, his place in the Do 335 test programme was taken by Flugkapitän Karl-Heinz Appel, who had joined Dornier as a test pilot in January 1939. An aviator of some experience, Appel had been involved with flight-testing the Do 17, Do 215 and Do 217, and had also been seconded to Greece, Yugoslavia and Bulgaria, all of whom had purchased Dornier aircraft pre-war.

In May two further prototypes, both fitted with DB 603A-2 engines, arrived from the factories. Do 335 V7 Wk-Nr 230007 CP+UG was flown for the first time on the 19th by Hans Dieterle when he took the aircraft from the Löwental plant to Mengen, where the Dornier would be engaged in exploring aileron development, performance measurements and testing equipment. The aircraft would also appear at Dessau, where it was used to test a pair of 1,715hp Jumo 213 engines. The V8, Wk-Nr 230008 CP+UH, was rolled out of Löwental and commenced ground trials on 22 May, before Hermann Quenzler took it into the air on the 31st. This aircraft was also involved in aileron tests as well as engine performance and temperature monitoring, being flown by Dieterle and Fliegerstabsingenieur Walter Baist from Rechlin. The V4 would be used for early night-flying trials (see Chapter Four), but it also suffered frequent damage to its undercarriage.

At a major conference on aircraft production held on 23 May 1944, Göring told Albert Speer, as well as Milch and other senior Luftwaffe officers, that he viewed the Do 335, along with the Ju 388, as being among those aircraft he considered 'capable of becoming future high-speed bombers', but that both types were 'really nothing more than fighter-bombers.' He did, however, recognize that an Achilles' heel was the lack of heavy armament for these types:

'The same aircraft could also assume the role of the so-called twin-engined or heavy fighter that is a heavily armed, long-range aircraft which does not carry bombs. In spite of all the present technical difficulties we must under no circumstances relax our efforts in the field of heavy armament; on the contrary, we must regard the 5cm cannon as the minimum heavy armament and produce a machine gun which has a really high rate of fire. This is still proving to be a disadvantage and we will not be able to manage indefinitely with the present calibre. All these roles can now be filled by aircraft of this one type, such as the Ju 388 or Do 335.'

It is clear that by this stage of the war, Göring viewed the Do 335 as one of the fundamentally required types in the Luftwaffe's frontline inventory:

'When I consider that one type of aircraft can be used as a high-speed bomber, long-range fighter, twin-engined fighter-bomber and so on, it appears that, excluding the jets, practically no other types except the Do 335 and Ju 388 will be required any longer. In brief, every contingency which I have mentioned can be met by four types, namely the He 177, the Do 335, the Ju 388 and the Ta 152.'

He was also of the opinion that the Dornier could be used as a torpedo-carrier, stating, 'I am convinced that the Do 335 would also be suitable for this task.'

On 7 June, Hitler ordered Hauptdienstleiter Dipl.-Ing. Karl-Otto Saur, the bluntly spoken head of the *Jägerstab* (a committee which comprised industrialists and representatives of the RLM that had been set up in February tasked with regenerating Germany's flagging and bomb-stricken fighter production), to accelerate production of the Do 335. A month later, on 6 July, Saur advised the *Jägerstab*:

'The Do 335 – another aircraft which is to be turned out in large numbers – is coming into production. This aircraft is a revolutionary innovation. Production will begin in November with one aircraft and another one in December, but will then increase to 100 by the middle of next year and to 350 by

A cheerful member of the ground staff uses the control lever to demonstrate the functioning of the folding access ladder on the Do 335 V8. The ladder retracted into its own bay in the wing root.

the end of the year. This output will remain constant, but another model will be produced giving a total output of 470 and subsequently 525 aircraft. These figures refer only to the twin-engined fighter type. However, a bomber version will also be produced commencing as early as August with one aircraft, then three and five, and reaching 120 by next summer. Production of a long-range reconnaissance version will commence in October with an output of three aircraft, then eight and 15, and reaching 55 by the middle of next year. Output will be maintained at this level, thus giving a total figure of 525. Four trainer-version aircraft of this type will be turned out and then production will be stopped.'

The mention of a reconnaissance variant this late in the war would have been of cold comfort to Generalmajor Karl-Henning von Barsewisch, the *General der Aufklärer* (General of the Reconnaissance Arm), who had suggested back in the spring deploying the Do 335 for badly needed long-range reconnaissance missions over Britain, particularly of the naval base at Scapa Flow and also London.

Do 335 V9 Wk-Nr 230009 CP+UI seen in profile at Mengen in July 1944. This aircraft was the parent of the ensuing A-0 series, and was used to conduct armament tests. It too was another machine that suffered from landing gear issues.

Four days after the *Jägerstab* meeting, the Do 335 V7 was flown from Löwental to Rechlin in order to carry out a demonstration for Generalfeldmarschall Milch, but on 13 June the aircraft suffered a broken undercarriage strut while taxiing. By this time, Milch was considering using the Do 335 to replace the Heinkel He 177 *Greif* (Griffon) bomber, which was proving both disappointing in performance and vulnerable in operations. One option was to switch the Heinkel assembly line at Oranienburg over to the Do 335 from February 1945 once He 177 production there had terminated. A target figure of 200 Dorniers per month was discussed for the Heinkel facility.

From the earliest stages of its design, the Do 335 was intended to be fitted with an ejector seat – one of the first piston-engined aircraft to be so equipped – and the V3 would carry the distinction of being the first prototype installed with the compressed air seat of Heinkel design, complete with a padded headrest, heel and arm rests. Indeed, the seat would be deployed in testing and operational conditions, but it was not known for its comfort or efficiency – post-war claims among the Allies that some German test pilots had lost their arms as a result of tests were untrue, however. Tests were carried out at the wind tunnel at Manzell in the autumn of 1943, initially using a wooden dummy. The seat was set at an angle of 13 degrees and test-launched pneumatically 200 times. It was concluded that ejection velocity could be improved by applying grease to the piston that pushed the seat at launch. Furthermore, the seat was found to be nose-heavy, a situation that was solved by installing more material around the head armour.

Following tests with a dummy in June 1944, a live volunteer was also used for manual operation of the seat, which required a somewhat cumbersome trigger process. A pilot would need to first depress a button on the right side of the cockpit that jettisoned the rear engine propeller. A second button would blow away the upper tail fin, while a third would do the same for the lower one. After that, he would unlock the canopy and jettison it, then disconnect his microphone. Then he was to raise a handle located on the right side of the seat up to its first level, before straightening his back in the seat and placing his feet on the seat edge. He would then move the handle to the up position and the seat would eject. After ejection, the pilot left the seat and deployed his parachute.

Do 335 V9 CP+UI was delivered in June and was intended as a prototype for the planned A-1 fighter-bomber variant. Referred to by this time as the *Pfeil* (Arrow), the V9 was first flown on 29 June by Quenzler. The aircraft had a redesigned undercarriage and canopy, which opened to the right. It was armed with two MG 151/20, each with 200 rounds, mounted above the front engine and a single 30mm MK 103, with 70 rounds, firing through the crankshaft of the same engine and its spinner.

The V9 was transferred to the *Erprobungsstelle* (Test Centre) Rechlin on 3 August, where the aircraft suffered the ignobility of its gear collapsing on landing – not an auspicious arrival or a good advertisement for the Dornier. Undaunted, however, Flieger-Oberstabsingenieur Harry Böttcher of Department E2 (aircraft evaluation) and the very experienced test-pilot Dipl.-Ing. Heinrich Beauvais, who specialized in fighters and *Zerstörer*, conducted tests in the aircraft on 15 and 17 August, respectively, with Beauvais at one stage attaining a speed of 760km/h and also flying in a mock engagement with an Fw 190, which the Dornier outperformed with ease.

V4 Wk-Nr 230004 CP+UD finally took to the air on 9 July, its completion held up as a result of the complexity surrounding the larger Heinkel-designed high aspect ratio wing with which it was fitted, and which was intended for future development of the Do 335. The wing had a span of 18.4m and an area of 45.5m². The aircraft had only been in the air for 35 minutes when pilot Hans Dieterle became aware that, in a repeat of the problem that had plagued the V2 in April, the rear engine of the V4 had caught fire. Despite this, Dieterle managed to get the Dornier safely back on the ground. The aircraft was checked and repaired, and flight-testing commenced on 6 August at an unidentified location, possibly Rechlin, and lasted through to October, covering stability, wings, ailerons and engine cooling gills. After completion of the tests, the V4 returned to Löwental.

The Do 335 V5 was finally tested at Rechlin in early August, after which it was handed over to the Luftwaffe's armament *Erprobungsstelle* at Tarnewitz towards the end of September, where firing trials took place under the overall direction of Oberstleutnant Maximillian Bohlan and Walter Segitz. At Tarnewitz the V5's MK 103 cannon proved problematic, being prone to jamming in flight, and although some 1,400 rounds had been test-fired by the end of November, it was still not fully satisfactory. By comparison, the twin MG 151s worked well. There were also problems with the aircraft's undercarriage.

Production was affected – albeit briefly – following a raid by B-24s of the USAAF's Fifteenth Air Force on Friedrichshafen on 20 July which inflicted considerable damage on the assembly halls and workshops at Löwental. The first Do 335A-0, Wk-Nr 240101 VG+PG, was destroyed and this necessitated the move of the subsequent A-0s, Wk-Nrs 240102 and 240103, to Mengen for

A bad start for the next generation. Do 335 V11 (A-0) Wk-Nr 240111 VG+PO was one of a pre-production batch of aircraft to be converted into two-seat, dual-control trainers, but it suffered at least two nosewheel collapses at Oberpfaffenhofen in the early winter of 1945. Note the last three digits of the aircraft's Werknummer applied to the upper tailfin.

further work. Wk-Nr 240102 flew for the first time from the latter site on 30 September, and it was transferred the following month to Oberpfaffenhofen and later to Rechlin.

On 22 September 1944 the RLM issued a revision to its latest production plan to allow for the manufacture of some Do 335 two-seat, dual-control trainers. The first of these, the A-10, was to be based on a conversion of the airframe and general construction of the A-1 and to be produced by Dornier at Löwental, while 70 A-11 models, also based on the A-1, were to be converted at the Luther-Werke at Braunschweig, where A-12s would also be produced based on the specification of the envisaged B-6 nightfighter. At the end of September the first two examples – actually the second and third – of the Do 335A-0 became ready (the first, as mentioned, having been destroyed by the USAAF). Wk-Nr 240102 VG+PH and Wk-Nr 240103 VG+PI both carried out their maiden flights on the 30th and were then transferred that same day from Mengen to Oberpfaffenhofen by Hans Dieterle. By 20 November both machines were at Rechlin.

On 12 October, the V7 made its last known flight with Oberleutnant Josef Eisermann of the *Erprobungsstelle* Rechlin's Department E5 (navigational equipment and electrics) at the controls, but it suffered a burst tyre on landing, the resulting crash inflicting severe damage.

By the autumn, Dornier at Oberpfaffenhofen had also rolled out its first Do 335, A-0 Wk-Nr 240104 VG+PJ. It took nearly three weeks for the aircraft to make it as far as Rechlin for assessment following a forced landing at Dessau as a result of a lack of sufficient fuel load and the breaking of a hydraulic line. This was somewhat ironic as the purpose of this aircraft's tests at Rechlin was to assess hydraulics, oil temperature and landing gear issues, as well as weapons and radio equipment. VG+PJ was joined at Rechlin by A-0 Wk-Nr 240105 VH+PK on 10 December. This aircraft also had a problematic journey to the test centre, having been afflicted by a coolant leak that forced it to land at Illesheim. Once repaired, the pilot had to abort his first attempt to get to Rechlin because of bad weather.

Over the course of six weeks, three more A-0s flew to Rechlin: Wk-Nr 240107 VG+PM arrived at the *Erprobungsstelle* on 31 December, followed by Wk-Nr 240108 VG+PN and the final example of the A-0 batch to be produced, Wk-Nr 240110 VG+PP, which flew in on 9 February 1945. The latter aircraft subsequently suffered from undercarriage problems a few days later.

The ninth machine, Wk-Nr 240111 VG+PO, which was used for speed, climb and descent tests, remained at Oberpfaffenhofen, having sustained a badly damaged fuselage following a heavy landing there.

In late December 1944, the Do 335 V3 was still being used by Siemens to assess the best mounting methods for FuG 218 radar.

Stabsflugführer Robert Mossbacher was at the controls of Do 335A-0 Wk-Nr 240106 VG+PL when it embarked on a test flight from Oberpfaffenhofen on the wintry day of 20 February 1945. The aircraft had flown for the first time in December. However, on this occasion, it was another case of a DB 603 engine catching fire – this time the forward unit. Mossbacher was flying the big aircraft back to the factory airfield when he reported the fire by radio, but the prevailing fog is believed to have been his nemesis and he crashed near Unterbrunn, four kilometres from Oberpfaffenhofen. Mossbacher had not attempted to bail out and was killed.

Having conducted tests on several Do 335s in late 1944 and early 1945, the *Erprobungsstelle* Rechlin found that the type suffered regular problems and faults with its undercarriage and hydraulics, the latter particularly relative to both the main wheels and nosewheel. In a fair post-war assessment for the Allies, the *Kommandeur der Erprobungsstellen* (Commander of Test Centres), Oberst Edgar Petersen, summarized his views on the Do 335:

'When the Do 335 was constructed, flight tests produced a maximum speed at sea level of 612km/h and 730km/h at 8,000m, but the following difficulties were brought to light:

(a) The aircraft was unstable about its lateral axis and landing was difficult.

(b) The rear engine was prone to catch fire.

(c) The rear airscrew shaft constantly failed, though this was remedied by the substitution of spring gears for spur gears.

(d) The undercarriage and hydraulics were far from satisfactory.

(e) There was appreciable difficulty with the compass installation.

'In addition to these troubles inherent in the design of the aircraft, development was impeded by constantly conflicting instructions from high command as to the purpose for which the aircraft was to be used. At various times the design had to be revised for use as a fast bomber, a long-range fighter, a reconnaissance aircraft and a nightfighter.'

CHAPTER FOUR

OPERATIONAL TRIALS

On 26 April 1945 Do 335 V9 Wk-Nr 230009 CP+UI was flown by Fliegerstabsingenieur Heinz Fischer from Rechlin towards Switzerland, but the pilot was forced to bail out as a result of fuel shortage and the aircraft crashed in the Vosges mountains.

By the autumn of 1944, the immediate problem facing the Luftwaffe was a lack of sufficiently trained pilots able to defend the skies over the Reich or the Western Front by day and night. However, the Western Front had so deteriorated by this stage that neither Generalfeldmarschall Walter Model, the *Oberbefehlshaber West*, or his replacement, Gerd von Rundstedt, were able to stem the rapid pace of the Allied advance. Virtually unopposed, the troop-laden armour of the British Second Army broke out of France and swept on into Belgium, taking Brussels and the key port of Antwerp with its vital harbour installations still intact in early September. By late October, Montgomery's troops had reached the southern banks of the Scheldt, where the task was to flush the estuary of resistance so as to open Antwerp to Allied shipping. Worse still, in mid-September and further to the east, the first American troops had crossed the Sauer north of Trier and penetrated the frontier of the Reich itself. Two weeks later, elements of the American First Army breached what was thought to be the impenetrable Siegfried Line north of Aachen. The Front was collapsing and the Allies were now fighting within the borders of the Reich itself.

In the air, the strategic bomber offensive ground on, targeting the Reich's cities, industrial centres and transport network. The Luftwaffe fighter force struggled to put up any meaningful defence and the much-vaunted jet fighters had only just started to appear in tiny numbers.

In September, away from the enemy advance in the West, in the relative safety of the RLM in Berlin and the design offices at Dornier's plants at Friedrichshafen and Oberpfaffenhofen, a list of planned Do 335 sub-types had been drawn up that illustrated the varied roles

The unusual mix of curves, edges and angles that made up the Do 335 are seen to advantage in this view of Wk-Nr 240107 VG+PM (one of the ten A-0 pre-production machines) at Oberpfaffenhofen. Intended as a fighter trials aircraft, it was fitted with a single 30mm MK 103 cannon firing through the forward engine spinner and two cowling-mounted 20mm MG 151/20s. The stencilling on the fuselage above the supercharger intake reads, when translated into English, 'Disconnect Fire Extinguisher Pipes Before Removing the Panel'.

foreseen for the aircraft. The A-series was to run to ten variants (with most construction taking place at the Oberpfaffenhofen area factories) as follows:

A-1: Single-seat bomber or *Zerstörer* (destroyer), fitted with DB 603E-1 engines, with capacity for 500kg of bombs carried internally. Planned production run of 286. Revi 16D reflector sight. Blind-landing equipment (FuG 125) fitted. *Rüstsatz* (auxiliary fitments) possible for 2 x ETC 501A-1 underwing bomb racks for either 250kg bomb or 300-litre drop tank.

A-2: Single-seat *Kampfflugzeug* (bomber) – possibly with inclusion of enlarged wing and/or DB 603G or L engines. Construction by Luther-Werke at Braunschweig. 1,000kg bombload.

A-3: Planned single-seat reconnaissance aircraft, modified from A-1, with camera installation. Later abandoned. A sub-variant with enlarged wing also considered. Fitted with GM 1 (nitrous oxide) and MW 50 (methanol water) power boost.

A-4: Single-seat reconnaissance aircraft with smaller camera installation of 1 or 2 x Rb 50/18 cameras in fuselage bay.

A-5: Planned first single-seat nightfighter converted from A-1. Later abandoned. A revised plan produced as single-seat nightfighter and bad weather *Zerstörer* with enlarged wing. As alternative to Oberpfaffenhofen, Heinkel at Oranienburg was considered. Possibly considered for fitment with Jumo 213 engines.

A-6: Two-seat nightfighter converted from A-1.

A-7: Assigned variant for A-6 nightfighter with enlarged wing and DB 603L engines.

A-8: Assigned variant for A-4 reconnaissance aircraft with enlarged wing.

A-9: Assigned variant for A-4 reconnaissance aircraft with enlarged wing and DB 603L engines.

A-10: Two-seat trainer version. Construction at Friedrichshafen.

The planned new B-series, with increased armament and armour protection, consisted of the following variants:

Do 335 V3 Wk-Nr 230003 T9+ZH of the 1./*Versuchsverband* OKL (formerly V3 CP+UC) taxies out watched by a civilian official, possibly at Oranienburg in the summer of 1944. This aircraft was the only one of its kind to have a light blue-coloured ventral fin and radiator intake.

B: (no sub-variant number shown) *Zerstörer* – later abandoned.

B-2: *Zerstörer* fitted with two additional MK 103 cannon in the wings. Also two 315-litre drop tanks. Additionally, sub-variants planned for enlarged wing, DB 603L engines and pressurized cockpit, but all were abandoned. Construction at Oberpfaffenhofen and/or Heinkel at Oranienburg.

B-3: *Zerstörer* with enlarged wing.

B-4: *Zerstörer* with enlarged wing and DB 603L engines. Also pressurized cockpit proposed, but later abandoned.

B-12: trainer. Also proposed with pressurized cockpit, enlarged wing and DB 603L engines but eventually abandoned. Construction by Luther-Werke at Braunschweig.

By November, these intentions had changed slightly with what appears to have been the removal from the programme of the planned A-4 variant.

By the middle of 1944, Dornier was aware that the Luftwaffe was eager to evaluate the Do 335 as a nightfighter, the aircraft being seen as a potential replacement for the Bf 110 and even the Ju 88G. On 2 June Do 335 V8 CP+UH was duly transferred from Löwental to Mengen, where, in late July, it was fitted with experimental Fla-V flame-dampers for assessment as part of the nightfighter trial programme. Ground-testing with the flame-dampers continued at Mengen until 15 August. Relocating to Neuburg-an-der-Donau, the aircraft made its first night flight on 18 August, and further tests continued until October, including some at high altitude to properly monitor the dampers.

The other requirement, apart from bombing, was reconnaissance, especially over southern England, in order to monitor the strengths and movement of Allied forces intended for operations in France. In July 1944, expressly for this purpose, the Do 335 V3 was fitted with an experimental Rb 50/30 camera installation and delivered to the Luftwaffe's 1./*Versuchsverband* OKL (the testing and evaluation unit of the Luftwaffe High Command), based at Oranienburg, as T9+ZH, where it was flown on a few occasions by Leutnant Wolfgang Ziese, a former test pilot with the Siebel Company at Halle. Overheating

INSIDE THE DORNIER Do 335 M(V)13 WK-NR 230013 RP+UP

1. MK 103 cannon port (cannon not always fitted)
2. Forward DB 603E-1 engine and coolant tank
3. Engine bearer
4. 30mm MK 103 cannon
5. MK 103 ammunition canister
6. Accumulator
7. Retracted nosewheel
8. Lubricant tank – 45 litres (one fitted each side: left = forward engine / right = rear engine)
9. Main fuel tank – 1,230 litres
10. Secondary fuel tank
11. Rear DB 603E-1 engine
12. Fire extinguisher
13. Airscrew extension shaft (hollow)
14. VDM airscrew – 3.3m diameter

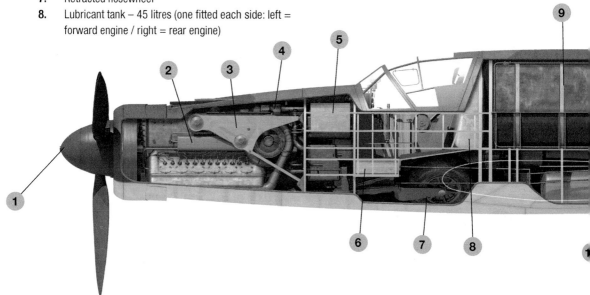

problems with the rear engine prevented any operational sorties being made and it is doubtful that Ziese ever flew over southern England in the aircraft. The Do 335 was eventually returned to Dornier for further tests.

However, of ever greater necessity was the need for faster, more heavily armed nightfighters to defend the Reich against the aircraft of RAF Bomber Command, and to this end, Dornier was instructed to prepare Do 335 V10 Wk-Nr 230010 CP+UK for nightfighter trials. This aircraft was modified by Ernst Heinkel Aktiengesellschaft (EHAG) at Wien-Schwechat to incorporate accommodation for a second crew-member, positioned behind and higher than the pilot and enclosed by a more raised canopy with clear vision panels.

Meanwhile, on 20 November 1944, an updated specification for the proposed Do 335A-6 nightfighter was issued. Similar to the A-1, the DB 603E-powered A-6 also incorporated accommodation for a second crew-member, who would act as radar operator, positioned behind and higher than the pilot beneath a more curved canopy. Like the pilot, he too would be strapped into a Heinkel ejector seat. In order to make space to accommodate the second cockpit, Dornier had to reduce the Do 335A-6's main tank capacity from 1,230 litres to 600 litres. However, the aircraft's overall fuel load was boosted by the installation of two 300-litre tanks into the wing leading edges. Two

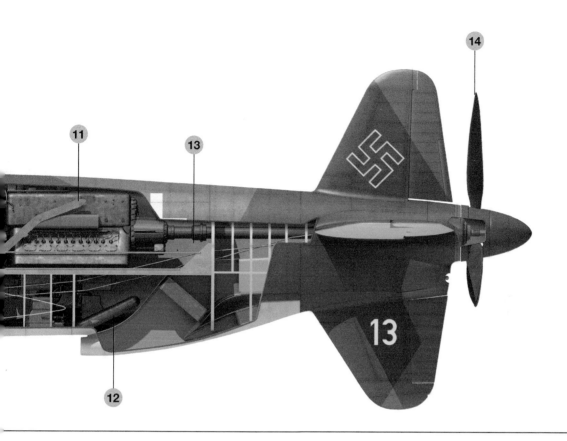

tanks for MW 50 were also built into the wings, the injection of which would boost the engines to 2,000hp when needed. Further fuel could be carried in 300-litre drop tanks under the wings. All this combined meant the total fuel load would equate to 2,320 litres.

Communications would be served by a Lorenz FuG 15 R/T and an EiV 15 intercom amplifier, while the aircraft would also be fitted with an impressive range of electronics, including a GEMA FuG 25a *Erstling* IFF set, the newly developed Lorenz FuG 125 *Hermine* VHF radio beacon signal receiver and a Siemens FuG 120 *Bernhardine* radio beacon receiver and blind landing set which recorded received information over a range of up to 400km at 5,000m in code on a strip of paper printed out from an attached teleprinter.

For combat purposes, the A-6 was to be fitted with FuG 220 SN-2a *Lichtenstein* airborne interception radar. Manufactured by Telefunken from September 1943, the *Lichtenstein* comprised two cathode ray indicators and a superheterodyne receiver. The transmitter and receiver connected together to the external aerials via a deflector and phasing unit. The internal equipment weighed 70kg. The four dipole aerial antennae were fitted into the leading edges of the wings. This unit was to be replaced later by the FuG 218 *Neptun* V radar developed jointly by Siemens and the *Flugfunkforschungsanstalt* (Aviation Radio Research

DORNIER Do 335 FROM ABOVE

1. Pitot tube
2. Left wing fuel tank
3. Oxygen bottles
4. 30mm MK 103 cannon
5. Cannon muzzle
6. Cannon fairing
7. Ammunition feed chute
8. Supercharger intake
9. Rear view mirrors in glazed blisters (left & right)
10. Supercharger intake
11. Ammunition boxes (l & r)
12. Retracted mainwheels (l & r)
13. Hydraulic fluid tanks (l & r)
14. Right wing fuel tank

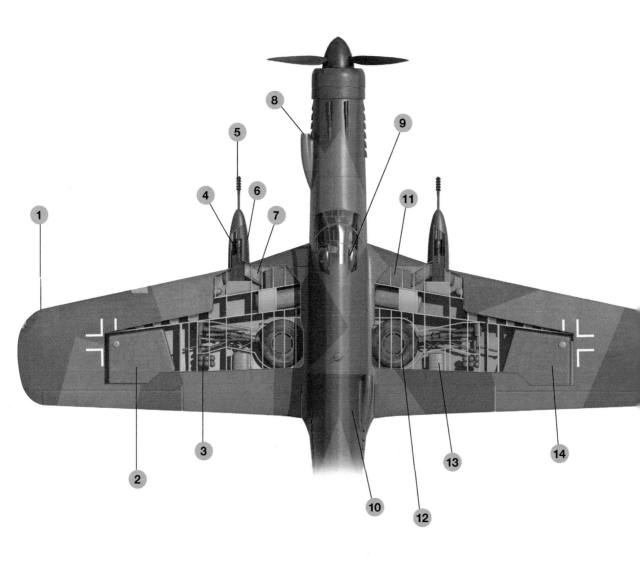

Establishment) at Oberpfaffenhofen and manufactured by Siemens. The FuG 218 *Neptun* V operated on higher frequencies.

In addition, the Telefunken FuG 350 *Naxos* Z passive radar was fitted, which functioned by picking up emissions from the RAF H2S set. The rotating aerial for this device was to be housed in a teardrop blister in the radar operator's canopy. The aircraft also boasted a Siemens FuG 101 radio altimeter.

The A-6 was to be armed in a standard configuration with an MK 103 cannon and two MG 151/20s, while internal ordnance could be carried in the form of a 500kg bomb instead of a 500-litre auxiliary fuel tank.

The aircraft was to be fitted with a sophisticated de-icing system (to be trialled on the A-05), the EZ 42 gyroscopic gunsight (to be trialled on the V13) and the Messerschmitt P8 high-speed reversible-pitch propeller that reduced the taxiing run by around 200m at maximum landing weight (to be trialled on the A-08).

It was calculated that the second seat, radar equipment and the installation of flame-dampers would reduce the aircraft's top speed by around 70km/h.

Despite all this extra equipment, somewhat surprisingly, the Do 335A-6 weighed just an additional 90kg over and above the A-1, with external dimensions remaining the same.

Flight tests with the Do 335 V10, which had been fitted with FuG 220 SN-2a *Lichtenstein*, commenced at Diepensee on 24 January 1945. The dipoles had been arranged so that the vertical antennae for lateral beams were on the left wing and the horizontal for vertical beams on the right. The aircraft had a standard canopy over the second seat and there was no blister, as intended in the original specification, for the *Naxos* set.

Another aircraft, the V16, fitted with FuG 218, was to have joined the nightfighter trials at the *Erprobungsstelle* Werneuchen on 25 January. This facility, under the command of Major i.G. Cerener, was responsible for developing day and nightfighter defence techniques and

Test pilot Leutnant Wolfgang Ziese who, in the summer of 1944, flew Do 335 V3 Wk-Nr 230003 as T9+ZH with the 1./*Versuchsverband* OKL at Oranienburg on operational reconnaissance trials.

Do 335 M(V)17 Wk-Nr 230017, which served as the nightfighter prototype, was uncompleted by war's end and taken over by the French at Mengen for examination and testing. A B-series airframe, the aircraft was provided with a seat for a second crew member located behind the pilot who, unlike in the twin-cockpit trainer version, sat at the same level as the pilot to function as radar operator with a FuG 220 set and other equipment. A small glazed panel was installed above the seat, which was accommodated by reducing the size of the fuselage fuel tank. The aircraft was flown in several post-war airborne and static ejector-seat tests by the French prior to finally being scrapped in March 1949.

fighter control, as well as the testing of radar, new jamming equipment and methods of electronic warfare. However, delays in production at Siemens meant that delivery of the V16 was postponed until early February, while the V15, V21 and V22 were also assigned as prototypes for the A-6. The V15, which had first flown on 31 October, had a second seat installed and wing aerials intended for FuG 218, which underwent some considerable testing.

The same day that the V10 arrived at Diepensee, a meeting was convened by the *Entwicklungssonderkommission Nacht- und Schlechtwetterjagd* (ESK-*Nachtjagd* – Special Commission for the Development of Night and Bad Weather Fighters), a commission based in Berlin under the chairmanship of Professor Kurt Tank. Representing Dornier, Claude Dornier's son, Peter, advised the commission that EHAG Nord at Oranienburg would be able to commence work on the first 50 A-6s, all fitted with FuG 220 SN-2d which had its dipoles arranged diagonally at 45 degrees in order to improve functioning while operating against 'Window' jamming by narrowing the beam width, in March 1945. This was later revised to 30 A-6s before switching over to production of the B-6 fitted with DB 603LA engines and increased wing area of 41sq m.

However, some members of the commission voiced scepticism over the Do 335's potential as a nightfighter. In their view, the high costs of manufacturing the Dornier precluded any further investment, there was no operational experience with it, its performance in the climb and maximum speed were already exceeded by the new jets and there was no provision for centimentric air interception radar in the nose. Although the RLM was at odds with these views, having slated the Do 335 as 'the' nightfighter for 1945, Professor Tank was of the opinion that the aircraft would only be adequate until mid-1945, after which the Messerschmitt Me 262 and Arado Ar 234 could operate as nightfighters until such time as an appropriate three-seat nightfighter came on stream.

Dornier refuted such a view and responded with a torrent of technical data to counter the ESK-*Nachtjagd*'s assertions, as well as still further proposals. Dornier argued that, in fact, a powerful piston-engined fighter would be of superior performance to a jet aircraft in terms of endurance and would require less take-off distance.

When it came to maximum speed, the Do 335 was equal to the main prevailing threat which was the Mosquito. Indeed, by adopting a laminar-flow wing, maximum speed could be increased to 750km/h. Apparently thinking on his feet, Dornier also proposed replacing the rear DB 603 engine with a HeS 011 turbojet unit, claiming that when so equipped, the Do 335 would be able to maintain a speed of 760km/h for two hours – a notion that bewildered the commission. As for the issue of centimetric radar, Dornier advised that an alternative device would be built into the wings, and if this proved inadequate, a centimetric radar was incorporated in the submission for the proposed Do 435 *Zwilling* that had already gone to the RLM for consideration.

But none of this went down well with the ESK-*Nachtjagd*, and Dornier was given the task of developing a jet fighter instead. Indeed,

The aggressive form of two-seat Do 335 V11 Wk-Nr 230011 CP+UL makes the aircraft appear as if it is ready to pounce on its prey directly off the ground. This machine first flew on 3 September 1944 with Karl-Heinz Appel at the controls, and it subsequently served as the prototype for the A-10 series of training aircraft.

it was noted in the handwritten draft ESK conference minutes that Peter Dornier 'treated the Do 335 like a propaganda exercise, praising the advantages of his aircraft over that of the jets.'

Running alongside the plans for, and development of, a two-seat nightfighter was the building of two-seat trainers, which would be required when the Dornier started becoming available in numbers for operational service. These variants were designated the Do 335A-10, A-11 and A-12. The principle was the same, but instead of a radar operator, an instructor would sit in the 'cockpit' behind the front (pupil) pilot, operating the main controls and with access to the main instruments. Again, to create space for the instructor meant a reduction in tankage to 355 litres in the main tank, which was 'L'-shaped to allow it to fit beneath the instructor's seat – the latter was of an ordinary, non-ejection type. To go some way to recovering lost fuel, the wing tank capacity was increased from 310 to 375 litres, providing a total fuel load of 1,105 litres. Despite the lack of powered escape, from his rear 'perch', the instructor benefitted from excellent all-round vision.

As the A-10, the aircraft was to be powered by DB 603A-2 engines, while the A-11 was to be fitted with E-1s. It is believed the A-12 would have been fitted with Jumo 213 units. A run of 20 A-10s was planned for conversion by Dornier at Löwental, while the Luther Werke at Braunschweig was to undertake conversion work for the A-11 and A-12.

The first trainer prototype, Do 335 V11 Wk-Nr 230011 CP+UL, powered by DB 603A-2 engines, took to the air on 3 September 1944 flown by Karl-Heinz Appel, the colossal aircraft gaining the moniker of *Ameisenbär* (ant-eater) on account of its humpback fuselage. On 11 October, flown once more by Appel, the V11 took part in a test that must have appeared as an impressive sight when it was accompanied in the air by the V8 flown by Stabsingenieur Walter Baist of the *E-stelle* Rechlin, who was to act as an observer from the rear. At a height of 800–900m, rather than jettisoning the V11's 200kg rear propeller on the troop training ground at Heuberg, for reasons of 'time

and fuel economy' Appel released it over Mangold airfield once the necessary safety measures had been quickly put in place. The test had been intended to assess the feasibility of such action in an emergency situation, bearing in mind the risk to the pilot of striking the propeller as he bailed out. For its part, on landing, the V8 overshot the runway and came to an inglorious stop in a potato field.

Three weeks later, in the freezing weather of 2 December, Appel had a close shave when, as he brought the V11 in to land, the aircraft failed to lose speed after touching down on a runway covered in ice and snow. A little earlier, a truck had crossed the runway and left 10cm-deep ruts in the snow. One of the aircraft's mainwheels hit one of the tyre ruts, breaking its axle, whereupon the Dornier skidded across the runway with one wing trailing along the ground as it headed, out of control, towards a line of parked trucks. Fortunately for Appel, who feared a collision and an explosion, the trainer slewed to a stop close to the vehicles. Shaken, but relieved, he clambered out and inspected the Dornier. The only damage was to the grounded wing tip and some buckling of the fuselage skinning.

Do 335 V12 Wk-Nr 230012 RP+UO was intended as a prototype for the A-11 variant, and as such it was fitted with DB 603E-1 engines and, at one stage, tested the Messerschmitt P8 high-speed reversible-pitch propeller intended to reduce the aircraft's landing run by a quarter.

On 1 December, Hauptdienstleiter Dipl.-Ing. Saur, who had previously headed up the *Jägerstab* and who now worked as Chief of Staff on the *Rüstingsstab* (Armaments Staff), visited Rechlin to attend a demonstration of the latest examples of aircraft, weaponry and equipment. As part of a display that included flights by the Me 262, Ar 234 and Ju 388, Saur watched a demonstration of the Do 335 V5 flown by Fliegerstabsing. Voigt of Department E-2. The fighter seems to have failed to impress, however, for in the ensuing aircraft production programme the Dornier was initially omitted.

During the middle of December, the RLM issued a revision to the aircraft designation system, calling for the termination of the 'V' numbers denoting experimental prototypes in favour of a new 'M' for

Nicknamed the *Ameisenbär* (ant-eater), Do 335 V11 CP+UL is seen here in profile, its twin-cockpit arrangement clearly evident. The second, rear cockpit was for the instructor, who was given clear all-round vision from his lofty perch. The aircraft was used to conduct trials in jettisoning the rear propeller up until it crash-landed on 30 December 1944 as a result of undercarriage failure, and it is not believed to have flown thereafter.

OPPOSITE
Do 335 M14 WK-NR 230014 RP+UQ, Oberpfaffenhofen, autumn 1944
This aircraft was intended to serve as a prototype for the B-2 *Zerstörer*, and as such it is fitted with 30mm MK 103 cannon, equipped with flash suppressors, housed in faired, wing-mounted pods. This aircraft also trialled the EZ 42 gyroscopic gunsight.

© Simon Schatz www.luftwaffe-profile.at

'*Muster*' (model) reference. This system was adopted to avoid confusion with the new *Vergeltungswaffen* (vengeance weapons), such as the V1 flying bomb and the V2 rocket, which were gaining increasing profile. However, while some facilities did adopt this practice, others did not, leading to confusion and inconsistency in designations and markings.

Forward view of Do 335 M(V)14 Wk-Nr 230014 RP+UQ, fitted with wing-mounted 30mm MK 103 cannon.

ENTER THE 'B'

As early as the summer of 1944, while still working on the overall concept for the Do 335A, Dornier commenced development of a new 'B' series, predominantly as heavily armed *Zerstörer* that would be able to carry some of the large-calibre weapons being created for deployment against Allied bomber formations. It was also hoped that such a fast, yet heavily armed, 'destroyer' could avoid or outperform the increasing numbers of enemy fighter escorts.

Eight versions were planned, the first – the B-1 – being a single-seat day fighter, similar to the A-01, but with an armoured windscreen and some revisions to equipment. However, it was the follow-on B-2 that initiated two prototypes being assigned as test aircraft for the new variant, the first of which was M(V)13 Wk-Nr 230013 RP+UP, which, powered by DB 603E-1 engines, made its maiden flight on 31 October 1944 with Quenzler at the controls. The aircraft was pre-armed with two wing-mounted 30mm MK 103 cannon, each weapon provided with 70 rounds and resting in extended fairings. To accommodate the cannon, the aircraft's 310-litre wing tanks were removed and replaced by smaller 220-litre tanks in the outer wing sections. Because of the added armour and armament, the B-2 required larger 840 x 300mm tyres and thus, in the case of the nosewheel, it had to rotate through 45 degrees when retracting.

M(V)14 RP+UQ was similar to the M13 in being fitted with an ESK 16 gun camera but also an EZ 42 gunsight. For many years, German fighter aircraft had been largely equipped with a simple reflector gunsight, but the EZ 42 would permit a pilot to fire at an airborne target without allowance for the movement from fixed guns built into the longitudinal axis of the carrying aircraft. When approaching a target, a pilot had to ensure that he continuously twisted

Rear view of Do 335 M(V)14 Wk-Nr 230014 RP+UQ at Oberpfaffenhofen.

the range-finding button on the aircraft's control column so that the growing target was permanently encapsulated in the dial, as well as making sure that the cross-wire was contained within the target-circle on the target. The precise angle of deflection was obtained within two seconds. Accuracy could be guaranteed to within 15 per cent of the angle of deflection in the longitudinal direction of the enemy and 10 per cent perpendicularly.

The M14 made its first flight in November 1944, but thereafter there were problems, including fumes from the guns leaking into the cockpit as well as synchronization difficulties.

It was intended that series production of the Do 335B would be undertaken by EHAG at Oranienburg, but various supply and tooling problems resulted in the first delivery not taking place until February 1945.

As development work continued, it was planned to re-engine the B with more powerful 2,000hp DB 603LA units as the B-3, which would also be fitted with an enlarged, 18.4m-span wing to improve performance at altitude, and standard armament of one MK 103 and two MG 151s. This variant was labelled as a *Hohenzerstörer* (high-altitude destroyer), and although Do 335 V18 and V19 were slated for development of this *Zerstörer*, neither fully completed prototype saw the light of day. Furthermore, difficulties at Daimler-Benz meant that delivery of the L-series DB 603 engine would not take place until the autumn of 1944.

If such aircraft had ever taken to the sky in numbers, there is little doubt that they would have given the bombers of the USAAF and RAF Bomber Command a battering. The combined firepower of up to three MK 103 cannon (one engined-mounted and two wing-mounted) and two 20mm MG 151s in the cowling would have delivered a significant punch. Furthermore, weapons specialists at the *Erprobungsstelle* at Tarnewitz were exploring the feasibility of arming the Do 335B with the new Rheinmetall 55mm MK 112 automatic aircraft cannon, which was essentially a scaled-up version of the proven 30mm MK 108 as carried by Fw 190 *Sturmjäger* units operating in the defence of the Reich.

The Do 335B-4 was planned as an *Aufklärer* (reconnaissance) aircraft, to be powered by the still-awaited DB 603LA engines and fitted with high aspect ratio wings, which would also be used by the B-5 trainer.

An initial batch of 50 B-6 nightfighters was to be built at EHAG Oranienburg, the first examples of which would be delivered in April 1945. This variant was based on the A-6, but had been improved structurally and featured a redesigned nosewheel. It was described in an overview of the aircraft dated 2 January 1945 as being 'distinguished by increased strength. The total fuel capacity is sufficient for a flight of 2.3 hours (with continuous power output at a maximum boost altitude). The optimum duration of flight with throttled down engines is 4.35 hours at an altitude of six kilometres and six hours at sea level.' Equipment would include FuG 220 SN-2 *Lichtenstein* in the first 30 machines, after which this apparatus would be replaced by the FuG 218 *Neptun* V radar.

Production targets for the B-6 were set at 12 for February, five for March, 20 for April and May, 50 for June, 75 for July and 100 for August, September and October. It is possible some examples of the B-6 may have been completed by EHAG at Oranienburg. As an uprated version of the B-6, the B-7 would be powered by DB 603LA engines, while the final B-8 variant was to have been a high-altitude nightfighter with a 43sq m wing area and also fitted with the same engines.

Other nightfighter prototypes had been planned: the M21 was booked to commence testing at Werneuchen on 10 February 1945, followed by the M22 a month later, while the M18, M19 and M20 were slated for long wingspan development, but if any such work progressed, it was destroyed before the end of the war. Also under consideration was the fitment of a *Schräge Musik* (jazz music) oblique armament apparatus of the kind which had been installed in Bf 110 and Ju 88 nightfighters with some success, intended for making attacks on RAF bombers from below. The intention was to calculate to what extent fuel load would be curtailed by such an installation, but it is not believed work progressed much beyond the preliminary stage.

LUFTWAFFE OPERATIONAL PLANS

The long-range, nocturnal reconnaissance squadron *Aufklärungsstaffel* 3.(F)/*Nacht* had been formed on 1 June 1941 equipped with Do 17s. One of the *Staffel*'s earliest bases is believed to have been Insterburg in East Prussia, from where it staged progressively to Kowno in July 1941 for the German invasion of the Soviet Union, then Pleskau, where at one stage it was assigned to FAGr. 1, then Riga-Spilve, where it was based from December 1943. At the beginning of that year the unit gave up its Do 17s and converted to the Do 217, its mission remaining long-range night reconnaissance of Soviet-held territory. On 15 May 1944, however, *Aufkl.St.* 3.(F)/*Nacht* was relocated again, this time to Brieg, in south-western Poland. On 30 June, word reached the unit that it had been assigned to commence training on the Do 335.

The following month, further orders reached the headquarters of bomber unit III./KG 2, based at Achmer under Major Albert Schreiweis, a highly combat-experienced officer who had flown the

Major Albert Schreiweis (centre, front row) and the officers and NCOs of *Erprobungskommando 335*, photographed in southern Germany in late 1944. This small *Kommando*, intended to carry out operational assessment of the Do 335 on behalf of the Luftwaffe, numbered no fewer than four Knight's Cross-holders, all of whom are seen here flanking Schreiweis in the front row. They are, from left to right, Leutnant Ernst Andres, Oberleutnant Joseph Steudel, Schreiweis, Hauptmann Alois Magg and Oberleutnant Peter Broich.

Do 217 in operations against England. Schreiweis had been with III./KG 2, as an oberleutnant, from at least May 1942. As a *Gruppe*, III./KG 2 had operated the Do 217 in bombing operations against Britain since January 1942 from bases in France and the Netherlands. On 13 March Schreiweis had been promoted to hauptmann and served as Technical Officer in the *Geschwaderstab*, but on 10 April 1943 he was appointed *Staffelkapitän* of 9./KG 2, a post which he held until 14 August when he took over command of III. *Gruppe* from Major Kurt Leythauser when the latter was assigned to the RLM.

On the night of 15/16 August, Schreiweis' Do 217M was hit by AA fire during an attack on Portsmouth and he was wounded. He managed to get back to France, but was forced to make an emergency landing at Evreux. On 16 January 1944, Schreiweis was awarded the *Deutsches Kreuz in Gold* (German Cross in Gold), followed by the *Ehrenpokal* (Honour Goblet) on 15 May. He had another close shave when, on the night of 17/18 June 1944, he had to bail out of his Do 217K after it ran out of fuel 24km north-east of Minden. A few days later, on 22 June, III./KG 2 was withdrawn from operations, detached from the tactical command of the IX. *Fliegerkorps* and returned to the Reich. On 4 July, the *Stab*, 9. *Staffel*, some technical personnel and six crews were ordered to Friedrichshafen for conversion training on the Do 335. This was the first step in accordance with a more general plan to establish four *Gruppen* of Do 335s by December 1945.

The assigned personnel of III./KG 2 were quartered in the barracks of a local flak unit in Manzell, and in preparation for the arrival of the rest of the *Gruppe*, Schreiweis was given the powers of a *Geschwaderkommodore*. Eventually, he found more permanent quarters for his unit in a camouflaged former army barracks in Langenargen on the shores of the Bodensee, not far from Dornier at Friedrichshafen. Over time, personnel from the *Gruppe* would relocate some 70km north to the airfield at Mengen an der Donau, where conversion training on the Do 335 was intended to take place.

There had been little preparation for the arrival of the men of KG 2, however, and basic accommodation was quickly found in a Hitler Youth home in nearby Ennetach. More frustration was to follow since delays and a lack of available Do 335s meant that, at first, no training was possible. However, following lengthy discussions with representatives of Dornier, Schreiweis took the somewhat radical, if not resourceful, measure of assigning his men towards assisting in the actual production of the Do 335 at the factories; if nothing else, that way they would truly learn about the new aircraft, as well as hopefully hastening its delivery to the Luftwaffe. The bomber crews had to learn to deal with constant interruptions in the supplies of parts and tools due to bombing raids, and a shortage of fuel meant that most deliveries and general transport associated with Do 335 production had to be effected with wood-burning vehicles – trucks powered by heating gas were also used.

On 15 October, it was decided that those elements of III./KG 2 no longer required at the airfield in Mengen would be transferred by rail back south to the town of Konstanz on the Bodensee, where they were to be quartered in a nearby school and assist in the local production of frames 20, 21, 22 and 23 for the Do 335.

Five days earlier, on 10 October, a new, dedicated test unit, *Erprobungskommando 335*, was formed at the Dornier facility at Mengen under the command of former reconnaissance pilot Hauptmann Hans Felde. Its primary objective was the assessment of the Do 335 as a military aircraft for fighter, bomber and reconnaissance purposes, familiarizing crews with it, listening to their reactions and preparing a Luftwaffe manual on the aircraft. The order to establish such a unit had been issued the previous month, on 4 September, with the intention of it remaining in existence for six months.

The core of the unit was formed from technical personnel from the *Erprobungsstelle* Rechlin, to whom were added a further 21 personnel from III./KG 2 and nine others from fighter and reconnaissance units. An indication of the importance with which the Do 335 was viewed at this stage is revealed in the fact that there were no fewer than four Knight's Cross-holders within the ranks of the small *Kommando*.

Oberfeldwebel Peter Broich had flown the Do 17 over France in 1940 with 3./KG 2, where, on 27 May, his aircraft was shot up by enemy fighters near Dunkirk and he was forced to make an emergency landing with wounded crew on board. A few weeks later, his Dornier was attacked on two separate occasions while making bombing attacks over England, and on both occasions he managed to make it back to France. Broich later saw action in Yugoslavia, Greece and Crete, often flying the most difficult missions. In 1943, he flew both the Ju 188

OPPOSITE
A page from the RLM's December 1944 Do 335A-1 handbook showing the intended operational standard camouflage splinter pattern to be used on the aircraft. Uppersurfaces were to be finished in RLM 81/82 Dark Greens while the propellers and spinners were in 70 Green and the undersides in 65 Pale Blue.

D. Aufbau des Baumusters

1. Die Bauteile

des Flugzeuges, auch Deckel, Leitungsschächte usw. sind durch Schilder, Einschlag oder Aufmalung der Sach- bzw. Zeichnungsnummer gekennzeichnet. Für Normteile gilt die jeweils vorgeschriebene Kennzeichnung.

Im einzelnen vergleiche hierzu die Ersatzteilliste.

2. Der Oberflächenschutz

wird vom Flugzeughersteller möglichst sorgfältig ausgeführt. Vor Aufbringung des Anstriches wird nach besonderen Angaben mit DKH-Spachtel 10018 A gespachtelt. Ein Sichtschutzanstrich nach Zeichnung 335 A-0 Bl. 10 ist vorgesehen, siehe folgende Abbildung.

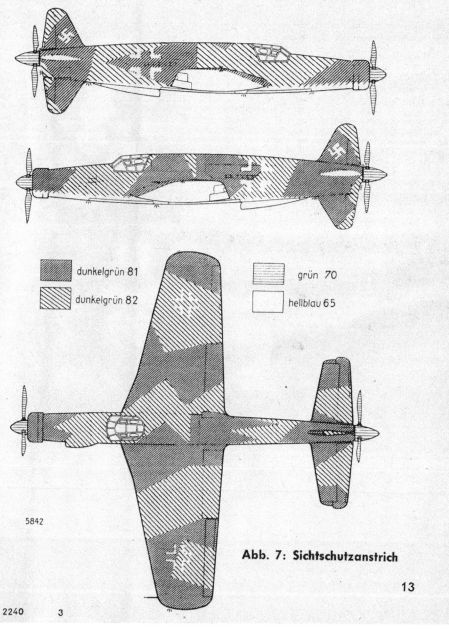

dunkelgrün 81

dunkelgrün 82

grün 70

hellblau 65

5842

Abb. 7: Sichtschutzanstrich

13

2240   3

and Do 217, and it was in the latter type that he was shot down by a British nightfighter near Le Havre on 29 July 1944. Broich had been decorated with the Knight's Cross on 27 March 1942 after 235 operational missions.

Leutnant Ernst Andres also flew the Do 217, making his first flight over England in the type on 31 August 1941. He was shot down by Spitfires during the British assault on Dieppe while he was attacking enemy landing craft, but he and his crew managed to bail out. Andres later flew with the *Geschwaderstab* of KG 2, and by early 1944 he had clocked up 100 combat missions over England. He subsequently participated in operations over the Invasion front as *Staffelkapitän* of 8./KG 2. Andres was awarded the Knight's Cross on 20 April 1944.

Hauptmann Alois Magg received the Knight's Cross on 5 September 1944. He had joined the Luftwaffe in 1935, and was a veteran of the Polish and Western Front campaigns. He was Technical Officer of I./KG 2 and flew several missions against Britain and over the Balkans. During Operation *Barbarossa*, he flew missions over the central and northern sectors of the front, but on 8 September 1941 his aircraft was hit by flak over Lake Ladoga and he was wounded. Nevertheless, Magg managed to fly back to base, where he made a wheels-up landing. Later, during 1942-44, he flew the Do 217 over England, mainly against London, then in operations against the Allied invasion. Magg made one flight in the Do 335.

Finally, Oberleutnant Joseph Steudel, like Broich and Andres, flew missions in the West and over England, attacking airfields and factories in the Do 17. He was wounded in air combat, but recovered to take part in operations over the Balkans and Crete, where he was involved in attacking enemy shipping. Steudel functioned as a Technical Officer and served at different times with 8. and 11. *Staffeln*. He also experienced several crash-landings following battle damage, and eventually took command of 8./KG 2. Steudel flew missions again against England from late 1943 through to the summer of 1944, after which he served as an instructor based in Hungary. He was awarded the Knight's Cross on 29 October 1944 in recognition of his record in operations against England.

These were the kind of airmen that were slated to fly the Do 335. On 11 November, those KG 2 personnel assigned to E.Kdo 335 became entirely independent of their former *Gruppe*. They would report directly to the *General der Kampfflieger*. In addition, the *Kommando* would be given a small *Zerstörerstaffel* for fighter assessment under a *Kommandoführer*, together with a maintenance section, whose main role would be to prepare the Do 335 for operations against the Mosquito. Reconnaissance assessment would be undertaken by a group of three pilots supported by 37 technicians under the command of a deputy *Kommandoführer*.

The maintenance crews also spent much of their time working with Dornier factory personnel, which was a perfect way for them to learn about the aircraft.

At one point, Major Schreiweis attended a briefing given by the *General der Jagdflieger*, Generalmajor Adolf Galland, and he gave him

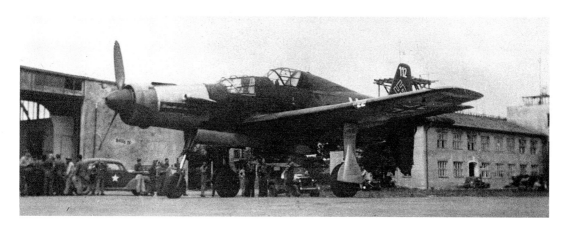

Two-seat trainer Do 335A-10 Wk-Nr 240112 at Oberpfaffenhofen, photographed shortly after the arrival of American forces. Aircraft such as this were intended to provide vital training for personnel from *Erprobungskommando* 335 and units such as III./KG 2 and *Aufklärungsstaffel* 3.(F)/*Nacht*, which had been slated to convert to the Do 335 for *Zerstörer*, bomber and nightfighter operations, respectively.

a copy of the new illustrated manual on the Do 335 that had been prepared by the personnel of III./KG 2. Galland leafed through the manual and commented that despite the Luftwaffe having so many different testing units, he felt that based on the manual, E.Kdo 335 would be the best. Schreiweis also took the opportunity to ask Galland whether, because it was extremely unlikely that the Do 335 would come to fruition in numbers in the near future, his *Gruppe* could be converted for standard nightfighter operations. Galland assured Schreiweis he would give the *Gruppenkommandeur's* suggestion thought.

Ultimately, no Do 335s were ever assigned to E.Kdo 335, and the unit's pilots made only a small number of familiarization and delivery flights using some of the prototypes and A-0 pre-production machines.

Schreiweis's proposal to convert what remained intact of III./KG 2 into a nightfighter unit was granted on 27 November, when the *Gruppe* was redesignated V./NJG 2 for equipment with the Ju 88G, effective 1 December. It was also decided at a conference on the same date that the original unit slated to take on the Do 335, the *Aufklärungsstaffel* 3.(F)/*Nacht*, should, instead, be re-equipped with the Ar 234 jet reconnaissance aircraft.

On 26 July the *Kommando der Erprobungsstellen* had authorized the establishment of '*Sonderkommando Nebel*' ('Special Detachment Nebel'), based at Offingen, under the command of Hauptmann Wolfgang Nebel. The unit was set up specifically to oversee the further development of the Messerschmitt Me 264 V2 and V3 ultra-long-range bomber prototypes, the so-called '*Amerikabomber*', and to assess the best use for them, the V1 having been destroyed in an air raid on Lechfeld in July 1944. The *Kommando* consisted of engineers and personnel drawn from the staffs of the *General der Aufklärungsflieger* (General of Reconnaissance Forces) and the *General der Fliegerausbildung* (General of Flying Training).

No sooner had Nebel's unit been established, however, than it was given fresh orders by OKL. It was to concentrate instead on the 'technical problems associated with new aircraft'; this meant not just the Me 264, but other new long-range types such as the Do 335 and the planned ultra-long-range Do 635 (see Chapter Five). To this end, the long-range maritime reconnaissance unit, *Fernaufklärungsgruppe* 5, based at Neubiberg, which, during the second half of 1944, had been operating four-engined Ju 290 patrol aircraft over the Atlantic from western France in support of the U-boats, was assigned the Do 335 (when available). The RLM advised the *Gruppe* that a two-seat version of the Do 335 was considered ideal, but a single-seat version would be acceptable for the required task. It was hoped that the former would have a range of 4,800km and the latter 5,500km, but this was more than twice that of the standard aircraft.

In December Rechlin finally made four Do 335s available to E.Kdo 335, but the deteriorating winter weather meant that only two pilots completed the required five–six hours' flying time over the course of the month. On the 24th, the *Kommando* suffered the loss of Feldwebel Alfred Wollank, a fighter pilot seconded to the unit, when the Do 335 V4 crashed at Bonefeld, near Koblenz, during a transfer flight from Oberpfaffenhofen to Rechlin. Wollank was killed. It is possible he had been attacked by an enemy fighter.

In a document dated 30 January 1945, the new *General der Jagdflieger*, Oberst Gordon Gollob, expressed his view that the Do 335 would make a good nightfighter. The following spring, sometime in March or April, Do 335 V10 CP+UK is believed to have been at Stade, where, as an A-6, it may have been intended for delivery to I./NJG 3 under Hauptmann Werner Baake – a unit that was also involved in assessing the new Ta 154 nightfighter. However, just two weeks later, on 14 February 1945, the continuing delays with the Do 335 forced the Luftwaffe to consider disbanding *Erprobungskommando* 335, but by 8 March it was still in existence, suggesting that someone, somewhere, high up in the RLM, or even higher, still had faith in both Dornier's capabilities as a manufacturer and in the aircraft they were working on.

Evidence that testing the Dornier continued into April 1945 lies in the fact that there are records of ejections. An Unteroffizier Bahlmann ejected from a Do 335 in April near Prague after he had observed that his rear engine was on fire. Unfortunately, once again the canopy fell back on the pilot after he had activated the bail-out procedure. Bahlmann somehow retained consciousness and pulled the eject lever, but nothing happened. In the meantime, it seemed as if the fire in the engine had receded and so he attempted a landing, but as he came down on the runway, the seat fired and Bahlmann was thrown out, suffering severe injuries in the process. The aircraft ran on to crash.

In the late afternoon of 26 April, Fliegerstabsingenieur Heinz Fischer was attempting to fly Do 335 V9 from Rechlin to neutral Switzerland. A compass fault took him erroneously into France and over the Vosges mountains. As his fuel supply ran down, Fischer decided to eject, but neither the tail jettisoning system not the ejector seat functioned and he was forced to bail out in the standard way with his parachute.

By late April 1945, the vice of the Allied armies to the west and the Soviet armies to the east was squeezing the lifeblood out of the Third Reich, metaphorically and literally. Despite the cataclysmic conditions, at the *Erprobungsstelle* Rechlin, as far as was possible, flight-testing had continued in some form, but preparations were being made to evacuate those aircraft considered important enough to be saved, even at such

Photographed at Oberpfaffenhofen after the plant's capture by the Americans, Do 335 M14 Wk-Nr 230014 RP+UQ is examined by German and US military and civilian personnel. The men on the wing would appear to be attempting to lower the extending access ladder. The M14 was fitted with a strengthened undercarriage and an EZ 42 gunsight, and served as a prototype for the planned B-2 series.

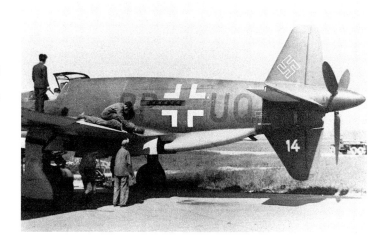

a late hour. To avoid capture by the Soviets, the options were either to fly west to Schleswig-Holstein or south to Bavaria or Austria and, if possible, to return such aircraft to their manufacturers. It was against this scenario that what was probably the last flight of a Do 335 in wartime was undertaken by Flieger-Haupting. Hans-Werner Lerche, a Rechlin test pilot.

Lerche had considerable experience in test-flying many types of German aircraft, as well as captured enemy aircraft such as the American B-17 Flying Fortress, B-24 Liberator, P-51 Mustang and P-47 Thunderbolt, the British Tempest V and the Soviet La-5 and Yak-3. Initially, he obtained authority to fly Wk-Nr 240104 VG+PJ, but the Dornier became unserviceable and the flight was called off. On 20 April, Lerche was ordered to fly Do 335A-03 Wk-Nr 240103 VG+PI south to Oberpfaffenhofen – a mission that suited him well since his girlfriend lived in the same area as the Dornier plant. It will be recalled from the previous chapter that Wk-Nr 240103 was first flown at the end of September 1944, and had been at Rechlin since November.

Lerche knew he would have to plan his route carefully as the Red Army was closing in on Berlin from the east and the north, so he elected to fly as far to the south-west of the capital as he could in order to avoid enemy fighters and flak. However, as he attempted to depart Rechlin that evening, the aircraft's nosewheel tyre burst as he was taxiing, the cause probably being an enemy bomb splinter from one of the numerous Allied bombing raids. Lerche was forced to abandon take-off. To replace such a tyre at this point was almost impossible. Fortunately, the partially fuelled A-02 Wk-Nr 240102 VG+PH was also at Rechlin, and at 1800hrs he took off without problem, heading for Lechfeld, the Luftwaffe training base to the south of Augsburg. Lerche was conscious that with the speed of the Do 335, landmarks such as railways and autobahns would be important. Nevertheless, it would still be a challenging navigational task.

After flying for a short time, Lerche realized that the aircraft's fuel pumps were not working, and as dusk approached, he decided to make an interim landing at Prague-Ruzyně, in Czechoslovakia.

He was forced to deploy the emergency pneumatic undercarriage lowering system when the main gear system failed. Shortly after first light on 23 April, Lerche took off once more. After an improvement in the weather, he followed a course along some forested Bavarian valleys, but as he records in his memoirs:

'Suddenly, tracer whipped past the Do 335 from behind. I still have no idea if this welcome came from the ground or from some enemy fighter, but it made me instinctively go into a violent evasive action, ram the throttles forward and plunge down almost to tree-top level.'

Instinctively, Lerche checked his instruments for signs of damage to the systems, but all seemed well. The engines continued to function normally, and Lerche concluded that it must have been ground-fire from advancing American troops in the area.

He kept the Dornier at a low altitude and headed south, crossing the Danube, the Alps appearing in the distance, to follow the railway lines towards Munich. Flying over Pasing railway station at 'telegraph pole height,' the Do 335 circuited Lechfeld airfield and landed there, where the pilot was informed that an air raid alarm had just been sounded and he would be lucky if the aircraft survived unscathed. Despite the subsequent Allied raid, VG+PH seemed to have a charmed existence. Refuelled, Lerche once more climbed into the Dornier and took off, bound for Oberpfaffenhofen, but as a precautionary measure he decided to leave the Do 335's undercarriage extended. As Lerche wrote:

'[A] few minutes later I landed my valuable aircraft intact at Oberpfaffenhofen and parked it nicely in front of the main building, to the surprise of the Dornier staff who could hardly believe their eyes.'

Lerche was fortunate to have survived his long flight. To the north, the Russians were less than 50km from Berlin. In reaction to a proposal from Göring that he assume full control of Germany should Hitler lose his freedom of action, the *Führer* dismissed the Reichsmarschall from all of his offices and ordered his arrest. A week later Hitler would be dead.

Do 335A-02 Wk-Nr 240102 VG+PH under tow at Oberpfaffenhofen in 1945 shortly after passing into American hands. The aircraft had undertaken a series of tests at the *Erprobungsstelle* Rechlin and was later flown alone by test centre pilot Flieger-Haupting. Hans-Werner Lerche back to the Dornier plant in late April 1945 – an accomplishment in itself given the level of Allied air superiority by that stage of the war.

CHAPTER FIVE

Ju 635

To take the weight of the Ju 635's enormous airframe, it was proposed to use the mainwheels from another large aircraft, the three-engined Ju 352 transport. Seen here is the Ju 352 V2 prototype pre-production machine, Wk-Nr 100029 CH+JB, photographed in the autumn of 1943. The aircraft was fitted with a ventral ramp known as a '*Trapoklappe*'. Most early examples of the Ju 352 saw service with *Grossraumtransportstaffel* 352, commanded by Oberleutnant Franz Lankau from March 1944.

In the late summer of 1944, it was realized by senior anti-shipping and reconnaissance officers in the Luftwaffe that the Focke-Wulf Fw 200 Condor and Junkers Ju 290 four-engined maritime bombers and patrol aircraft were becoming comparatively slow and outdated as the numbers and types of faster, longer-range Allied patrol aircraft and carrier-mounted fighters operating over the Atlantic increased.

As summer gave way to autumn and weather conditions at sea began to deteriorate, operations by the Ju 290s of the Luftwaffe's only dedicated long-range maritime reconnaissance unit, *Fernaufklärungsgruppe* (FAGr.) 5 '*Atlantik*', began to decline at just the time that the dwindling numbers of U-boats needed 'eyes' more than ever before to assist with searching for Allied convoys. However, by September 1944, Admiral Karl Dönitz, the commander of the U-boat arm, and Generalmajor Karl-Henning von Barsewisch, the Luftwaffe's *General der Aufklärungsflieger*, were forced to accept that with the imminent loss of vital airfields in France and the increasing superiority of the Allied air forces, the prospect of conducting any form of meaningful future cooperation between the Luftwaffe and the U-boats was very unlikely.

It was at this time that the *Gruppenkommandeur* of FAGr. 5, Major Hermann Fischer, began to spend less time at his unit's base at Neubiberg, to where his unit had relocated from Mont de Marsan in the summer, and more time in Berlin, where he worked with von Barsewisch and his staff to look at ways to recommence maritime air warfare against the Allies.

At a meeting at the RLM on 16 October, Fischer presented his requirements to representatives from Dornier, Heinkel and Junkers for

The mock-up of the proposed left-hand cockpit and canopy of the Ju 635. To the right, as viewed, is the main pilot's seat, while behind, facing aft, is the seat for the navigator/radio operator. He sat opposite his console, which was to have contained FuG 15 and FuG 200 'Hohentwiel' radio and radar equipment. Both crew sat under a revised canopy with a curvature similar to the Ju 188/288/388.

a strategic armed reconnaissance aircraft capable of conducting missions over the Atlantic with a range of 8,000km that could replace the Ju 290. This was to be based on the '*Zwilling*' concept as used by Heinkel in which the fuselages of two He 111 bombers had been mated together and used to provide power and range, for example for long-range air-towing, as had been done successfully in Russia. There was no reason why the same concept could not be used for long-range reconnaissance.

It was decided that the majority of such an aircraft should be used for fuel, although one fuselage was to be used to house 300kg of marker flares. The hope was that production should begin in January 1945, with one aircraft being delivered in that month, three each in February, March and April and four in May. The fact was that Dornier had already come up with its own plan for a Do 335Z, but at an early stage in the design process the company had handed its drawings over to Heinkel, which already had experience of such a concept following the creation of the He 111Z. Heinkel assigned the project number P.1075 to the Do 335Z, which comprised two Dorniers coupled together by a new wing centre section.

Work proceeded slowly at Heinkel, but on 12 October 1944, conveniently four days before the RLM meeting, the Junkers Flugzeugwerke seem to have taken over the P.1075 project to a great extent. The drawings were examined by Junkers' highly experienced Technical and Development Director, Professor Dr.-Ing. Heinrich Hertel, who felt that the design could be further modified and enhanced and – somewhat optimistically – a first prototype made ready as soon as February 1945.

Two days later, Junkers' designer Dipl.-Ing. Ernst Zindel gathered his engineering staff for a meeting to discuss the new project. They felt that the gap between the two fuselages and the small inefficient vertical fin would make flight following an engine failure difficult, that the fixed tailplane offered insufficient centre of gravity movement and that the

A view looking into the cockpit mock-up of the Ju 635 long-range reconnaissance aircraft/bomber. Facing left, as viewed, is the pilot's area, while facing right is that of the navigator/radio operator. This cockpit would have been built into the left-hand fuselage of the massive '*Zwilling*' (twin) arrangement.

Dornier-designed undercarriage of four retractable and two jettisonable wheels beneath the centre section was too complex. The project was also considered tail-heavy, but to counter this, one proposal was to use mainwheels from the big Ju 352 transport, as well as an additional, jettisonable wheel and a fuselage lengthened by eight metres.

By such measures, Junkers believed that it had the design for a radical new '*Zwilling*' concept for an Atlantic *Aufklärer* that would be able to assist the *Kriegsmarine* when it planned to resume a meaningful level of U-boat warfare in the late spring of 1945. The big Dornier, formed from the idea of mating two standard Do 335 fuselages to create more fuel capacity in a new wing centre section, was expected to possess a range of nearly 7,000 kilometres – enough at least to reach as far as the north of Ireland and the St Georges Channel. This would work ideally to Fischer's outline specification requirement for an ultra-long-range machine.

'EYES' OF THE U-BOATS

NEXT PAGES

The massive, menacing form of a long-range Junkers Ju 635 maritime reconnaissance aircraft of FAGr.5 ranges far out into the Atlantic, shadowing convoys for the U-boats in late 1946. Here, the Ju 635, which was essentially the '*Zwilling*' ('twin'-fuselage) concept for the Do 335 under Junkers management, conducts a rendezvous with a U-boat 'pack' prior to a convoy strike. The aircraft is fitted with large, underwing drop tanks and carries the emblem of FAGr.5 on the area below the cockpit – this marking had previously adorned the *Gruppe*'s Ju 290s. The Ju 635 is camouflaged in a typical scheme designed for over-water operations.

It was intended that the majority of the Ju 635's airframe should be used for carrying fuel, although there would be space within one of the fuselages for 300kg of marker flares. Had any of these aircraft been completed, they would have had the capability of flying nearly 7,000km – enough at least to reach as far as the north of Ireland and the St George's Channel from bases in western Germany.

On 25 October Dornier was ordered to produce a mock-up of the new fuselage, and on 1 November the company delivered a standard Do 335 airframe to Junkers for inspection. However, doubts persisted amongst the Junkers design and engineering teams about the viability of Fischer's 8,000km range requirement and the need for endurance of eight hours. It was recognised that one way to perhaps overcome these hurdles was to increase the depth of the wing centre-section to an astonishing 7.5m!

By early November Junkers was, effectively, in control of the *Zwilling* project, assigning it the project reference Ew 3670. Junkers soon renamed the project 'Ju 635' and received an order for four prototypes (the V1-V4) and six pre-production A-0 aircraft, with a plan that a series of 20 examples should be targeted, each with a range of 7,400km and a maximum speed of 680km/h.

During the first half of November a Do 335 arrived at Junkers' plant at Dessau and was flown by the firm's test pilot, Siegfried Holzbaur. He was not overly impressed by the Dornier, noting that its visibility to the rear was restricted, the flaps functioned too slowly and that the general handling and brakes were suspect.

Junkers revised the left fuselage cockpit area to include a second seat for a navigator/radio operator, with a Ju 388-style cockpit foreseen, while the right-side fuselage retained the appearance of a standard Do 355, carrying the second pilot and a fourth crewmember. The navigator and second pilot would operate the astronomical navigation equipment and the aircraft would carry oxygen sufficient for eight hours.

Notwithstanding Holzbaur's observations, Junkers pressed on with refining the Ju 635 design. The majority of the fuel load – 8,030 litres – would be carried in tanks in the wing centre and outer sections, while the fuselages carried another 5,810 litres, and although no armament was to be installed, the aircraft's left-side bomb-bay would be fitted with two Rb 50/30 cameras or one such camera and a 250-litre tank for GFM 1 power boosting, while the right fuselage would contain five 60kg flares.

On 27 November 1944, Major Fischer, now assigned to the *Chef der Technischen Luft Rüstung* (TLR – Head of Air Technical Equipment), together with Oberleutnant Hans Müller, FAGr. 5's Technical Officer, examined a mock-up of the new Ju 635 twin-fuselage *Zwilling* project. It seemed preliminary work on the enormous *Aufklärer* was well underway. After taking over the project, the Junkers design team had begun by installing FuG 16 ZY radio equipment in the left cockpit during late November/mid-December 1944, although it was later decided to revert to the FuG 15. The aerial was attached to the left-side dorsal fin. The loop for the *Peilgerät* 6 D/F set was attached beneath the left fuselage, where a FuBl 2 blind landing system was also mounted. A FuG 101 radio altimeter was fitted beneath the right wing. In addition, Fischer was informed that the FuG 200 *Hohentwiel* ship-search radar was to be supplemented, or replaced, with the new FuG 224 *Berlin A* target-indicating set.

Fischer and Müller expressed their satisfaction with the project, although as a result of their recommendation, the cockpit heating was

The small stowage area between the seats for the pilot (right) and navigator/radio operator (left) in the Ju 635 mock-up. The backs of the seats have been pushed forward. Visible to the right is the rear end of the pilot's left-side control panel, which housed the throttle levers, while in the foreground is an emergency flare pistol.

improved. The RLM asked that a large rubber dinghy be provided for emergency use over water, as well as the FuG 302 C 'Schwan-See' ('Swan Lake') droppable radio buoy developed by the *Flugfunkforschungsanstalt* (Research Institute for Aeronautical Radio) at Oberpfaffenhofen and the *Gesellschaft für Technisch-Wirtschaftliche Entwicklung* (Society for Technical-Economic Development) at Reichenau. This was a bomb-shaped buoy measuring 1,920mm in length and 470mm at its widest point, including its four tail fins.

The buoy, intended for U-boats to home on to, would be dropped vertically into the water, and on impact a telescopic rod antenna would extend from the end of the body that was exposed above the surface. After release, for a period of ten minutes, the aircrew could turn the transmitter on and off as a test and make minor adjustments. The beacon could then be set to transmit for up to 72 hours as it floated in the water. The crystal-controlled transmitter beamed at three watts on a fixed frequency, but the device was not always efficient.

In addition to this equipment, a senior official at the RLM also recommended that the Ju 635 be protected by the heaviest possible rearward-firing armament – a somewhat short-sighted suggestion given that the aircraft's greatest attribute would be its speed. Nevertheless, in an RLM document from 8 January 1945, it was proposed that four fixed, rearward-firing MG 151s, or *Ferngerichtete Drehringlafette* (FDL – remotely controlled turrets) 151Z, FDL-B or C 151Z be installed. An astounded Dipl.-Ing. Zindel protested that the Ju 635 should be able to rely on its speed to evade aircraft such as the Mosquito.

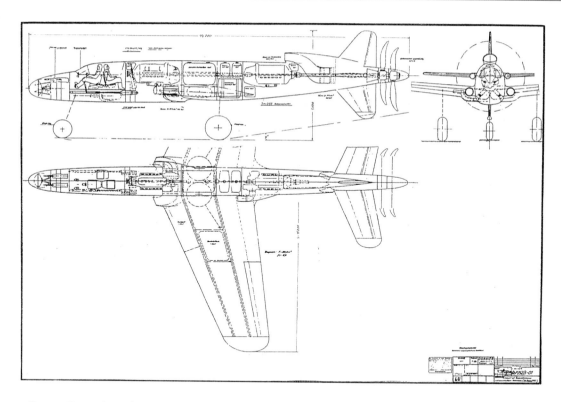

On 12 December, during a discussion between Reichsmarschall Göring, officials of the RLM and officers of the OKL, it was confirmed that four Ju 635s were on order, and that they would be built in Prague under the control of Junkers at Dessau. The *General der Aufklärer*'s request for the construction of 20 0-series pre-production aircraft was also in hand. It was felt that this could be achieved if a number of Do 335 fuselages were put aside in May 1945.

Development of the Ju 635 continued, but there were considerable delays. Scale models of the aircraft fitted with freely rotating propellers were used to conduct wind-tunnel tests, which revealed wing-tip airflow separation, but, oddly, only on one side. In the middle of January the *Chef* TLR reported that the order for additional machines over the four already sanctioned by the Reichsmarschall had been held up by labour problems at Junkers. It was envisaged that the first aircraft, which had been assigned for component testing and which was intended to be flight-tested in March, or the second aircraft, assigned for radio equipment trials, probably in June, would not become available until July/August. This was due to difficulties in the delivery of fuselages and a problem with the design of the wing. On 24 January, Göring again pressed for the production of ten Do 335s with two 300-litre or two 900-litre long-range tanks and 20 Ju 635s.

On 15 March, on orders from Hauptdienstleiter Dipl.-Ing. Saur of the *Rüstungsstab* and in agreement with Junkers, work on the Ju 635 continued, but on the basis of the simplest possible form of construction. However, no aircraft was completed before the end of the war.

A number of advanced 'push-pull' aircraft projects were proposed by Dornier. Seen here is a drawing of the proposed Do P 252/3 all-weather *Zerstörer* and nightfighter, which was to be powered by two DB 603LA or Jumo 213 J engines. It was to be armed with two 30mm MK 108 cannon that could fire forward or at an angle in the way of a *Schräge Musik* installation. A further pair of such cannon was to be installed below the forward engine. The aircraft was also to be fitted with the latest FuG 244 *Bremen* centimetric radar.

CHAPTER SIX

ASSESSMENT AND LEGACY

US military personnel, including a motorcycle dispatch rider on the left, gather to look at Do 335A-10 Wk-Nr 240112 (a two-seat trainer) at Oberpfaffenhofen shortly after the cessation of hostilities.

As victorious Allied forces flooded across the ruins of Nazi Germany from May 1945, so they came across countless examples of ingenious, technically advanced and radical German aircraft designs, from jet-propelled interceptors and bombers to manned flying bombs, tailless flying wings and semi-expendable fighter/bomber composite combinations. For its sheer size and curiosity, however, the Dornier Do 335 was second to none, and it generated considerable interest among Allied air-technical teams.

It was French troops who first discovered the aircraft when they reached the Dornier test fields at Löwental and Mengen, but they arrived to find only the burnt-out remains of aircraft. At Mengen, for example, there was the wreckage of the Do 335 V7 and the unfinished M17 nightfighter prototype.

The Americans got to Oberpfaffenhofen and found A-02 Wk-Nr 240102 VG+PH, which Flieger-Haupting. Hans-Werner Lerche (see Chapter Five) had flown there, as well as the M14. Jack Woolams, the renowned Chief Test Pilot at Bell Aircraft Corporation, undertook a detailed inspection of the Do 335s at Oberpfaffenhofen and was sufficiently impressed by them to recommend that two of them, VG+PH and A-1 Wk-Nr 240165, be flown to Neubiberg airfield by Dornier pilots for preparation for eventual shipment to the USA. Dornier technicians would also be assigned to assist in this task. The aircraft were subsequently flown to Cherbourg and loaded onto the Royal Navy carrier HMS *Reaper*, along with captured Me 262s, Ar 234s, Fw 190s, He 219s and a single Ta 152, having had their propellers removed before being

One of two plastic-wrapped Do 335s is lifted by crane on board the carrier HMS *Reaper* at Cherbourg in July 1945, bound for New York. The Dorniers were accompanied on their voyage by Me 262s, Ar 234s, Fw 190s, He 219s and a Ta 152.

shrouded in protective plastic for the voyage across the Atlantic to Newark, New Jersey.

Having arrived in the USA, the A-1 gave problems to its new 'owners'. On a ferry flight from Newark Army Airfield to Freeman Field, in Indiana, Woolams found that as soon as he was airborne, the temperature of the aircraft's rear engine rose dramatically 'until the needles went clear off the gauges.' Woolams flew the Dornier on one engine and landed back at Newark. He did so 'landing in a cloud of smoke and steam, with oil pouring out from the now badly overheated rear engine.'

In a cloud of dust, still carrying its German markings and with both DB 603 engines roaring, Do 335A-10 Wk-Nr 240112 taxies out watched by a US serviceman. The aircraft would eventually make its way to England as prized booty.

Do 335A-10 Wk-Nr 240112, in England and now adorned in British markings, attracts curious spectators while appearing at the German Aircraft Exhibition at Farnborough in late 1945.

The only Do 335 to make it to England, A-10 Wk-Nr 240112 was tested by the Experimental Flying Detachment at RAE Farnborough during the autumn of 1945. On 18 January 1946, while being flown by Gp Capt Alan F. Hards (the RAE's Commanding Officer of Experimental Flying), the Dornier crashed at Cove, a district neighbouring the test establishment.

VG+PH would end up with the Tactical Test Division at NAS Patuxent River, Maryland, from December 1945, and in the early 1960s the two 'American' Do 335s eventually ended up, in one form or another, at the Smithsonian Institution's Paul E. Garber storage and restoration facility at Silver Hill, also in Maryland. After a spell at the Deutsches Museum in Munich from 1976 following restoration by Dornier, VG+PH returned to the USA.

Like the Americans, the British also took two Do 335s from Oberpfaffenhofen – one A-10 two-seat trainer Wk-Nr 240112 and the other a single-seat model. In early September 1945, the A-10 was ferried by air from Neubiberg via Strasbourg, Reims and Manston to the Royal Aircraft Establishment (RAE) at Farnborough, where it was first tested by Lt Cdr Eric 'Winkle' Brown, a test pilot attached

to the Aerodynamics Flight of the Experimental Flying Detachment. He recorded:

'I found the Do 335 lively to fly, and right from the short take-off run under the smooth roar of the two Daimler-Benz DB 603s, it afforded

The Do 335 M17, believed to be Wk-Nr 230017, taxis at the CEV Bretigny in French markings, where it would be assessed in 1947.

Bearing French roundels and tail insignia, a view of the rear of Do 335 M14 Wk-Nr 230014, which had been captured at Mengen.

On 27 November 1948, the Do 335 M17, intended as a prototype for the B-6 nightfighter, suffered an ignobility at Bretigny when its starboard undercarriage retracted prematurely following a hydraulics problem during taxiing. The aircraft was pulled off the main runway and relocated to an isolated area of the CEV, where the airframe was relegated to static testing of the ejector seat. The M17 was eventually scrapped in March 1949.

that comforting feeling of being over-powered – a gratifying sensation that one seldom experiences. View in the air was excellent, and I had a distinct feeling that the Do 335 was better suited to nocturnal than diurnal fighting.'

The Do 335A-10 was one of the captured aircraft to be included in the German Aircraft Exhibition at Farnborough in November–December 1945, after which it made a further test flight on 15 January 1946, before being flown again on the 18th by Gp Capt Alan F. Hards, the RAE's Commanding Officer of Experimental Flying. Shortly after Hards took off, however, the A-10 began to suffer from the same problem that had afflicted the A-1 flown by Woolams in the USA, when its rear engine caught fire. Hards did not have radio contact with the ground, but as he came in to land he waggled his wings to indicate the need for an emergency landing. Hards was killed as the A-10 crashed at Cove in Hampshire.

The other, unpainted, Dornier selected by the British made it as far as Merville in northern France, where its pilot, Hauptmann Helmut Miersch, formerly with 2./FAGr.5, found he was unable to lower the nosewheel as he approached to land. Miersch duly feathered the front propeller and pressed the starter button, which allowed him to rotate the prop until he could land with the maximum ground clearance. However, no further attempt was made to fly the Dornier and it was scrapped at Merville.

Lt Cdr Brown summarized that:

'The Do 335 had certainly proved itself the most troublesome, mechanically, of the captured German aircraft tested at Farnborough, probably indicative of the fact that it had been committed to production before all its bugs had been wrung out. Despite all the trouble that it gave us, I was of the opinion that it would have made a highly successful nightfighter with its good stability, endurance and excellent turn of speed.'

The French took over two Dorniers at Mengen, M14 Wk-Nr 230014 and M17 Wk-Nr 230017, a prototype for the B-6 nightfighter. Having been repaired at Mengen, the M14 was flown to Bretigny and was then restored by the SNCASO factory in Surennes, before transferring to the *Centre d'Essai en Vol* (CEV) on 3 June 1946. The aircraft flew a number of times in 1947, which included flights with three MK 103s installed with ballast replacing ammunition, the last being on 4 March 1948. The M17 arrived at the CEV some months later and also flew during 1947, including making one bizarre flight in which the radar operator's seat was occupied by a dead deer that had been shot that morning, but the aircraft met its end in a forced-landing at Lyon-Bron.

With the demise of the Do 335, few aircraft adopted the push-pull engine configuration in the post-war years, although the American Cessna Model 336 Skymaster of the early 1960s did. The design of this twin-boom, six-seat, fixed landing gear, light utility aircraft meant that asymmetric handling problems were eliminated through centre-line thrust. It flew for the first time on 28 February 1961 and was produced in series between 1962 and 1964, a total of 195 Cessna 336s being manufactured. The subsequent Model 337 was taken on by the US Air Force in 1966 as the O-2 Skymaster, which had retractable gear and was used as a Forward Air Control and light observation aircraft. The California Department of Forestry and Fire Protection also used O-2 variants of the 337 Skymaster for fire-fighting operations from 1976 until the mid-1990s.

Do 335 M14 Wk-Nr 230014 undergoes extensive repair and restoration at the SNCASO factory in Surennes, near Paris, following a crash at Bretigny on 8 August 1945. The aircraft had developed the all-too familiar problem of its rear engine overheating and catching fire while being test-flown by a French pilot. The latter shut down the engine, but this had little effect, and in the ensuing emergency landing the aircraft's starboard tyre burst and it crashed into a parked B-26.

Survivor. Do 335A-02 Wk-Nr 240102 VG+PH was one of two Dorniers shipped to the USA at the end of the war. After many years in storage, it was acquired by the Smithsonian Institution in 1961 and placed in its Paul E. Garber storage and restoration facility at 'Silver Hill', Maryland, until airfreighted to Germany in 1974 and restored by Dornier at Oberpfaffenhofen. Company employees were astounded to discover the explosive tail unit jettison bolts were still intact when they stripped the airframe down. Displayed in the Deutsches Museum in Munich for a decade from 1976, the aircraft returned to the USA and went back into storage at 'Silver Hill'. In September 2005 the Do 335 was moved to the National Air and Space Museum's Udvar-Hazy Center in Chantilly, Virginia, and it is seen here on display – alongside an Arado Ar 234B-2 – in April 2013. (Richard Vandervord)

With the turn of the millennium, Denver-based Adam Aircraft Industries (AAI) developed the pod and boom A500, another six-seat utility aircraft using a push-pull configuration, with cabin pressurization and constructed mainly from carbon-fibre epoxy composite materials that featured a flame-resistant, meta-aramid Nomex honeycomb core. Again, the centre-line thrust was intended to reduce drag and maximize control of the aircraft should one engine malfunction or fail. The prototype A500 flew for the first time on 11 July 2002, but after a run of just seven aircraft, AAI ceased operations and filed for bankruptcy in February 2008.

Notwithstanding the limited success of aircraft such as the Cessna Model 336 and the A500, former Rechlin test pilot Flieger-Haupting. Hans-Werner Lerche summarized in 1976:

'The Do 335 was an unusually powerful aircraft with exceptional flying qualities, and an aeroplane that bestowed on me the pure pleasure of flying, a feeling which I shall not forget as long as I live.'

BIBLIOGRAPHY

DOCUMENTS

ADI(K) Report No.377/1945 *The life and work of Edgar Petersen*, 22 August 1945

AIR20/7708: AHB.6 Translation No. VII/124 – *Extract from report of the Goering Conference on Aircraft Production Programme*, 23 May 1944

AIR20/7709: AHB.6 Translation No. VII/137 *Fighter Staff Conferences 1944*

Royal Aircraft Establishment, Farnborough, Foreign Aircraft: *Dornier 335, Structural Features* by D. B. Cobb, Technical Note No. FA.264/1, July 1946 (via J. Richard Smith)

Various reports issued by the *Erprobungsstelle* Tarnewitz, 1944-45

BOOKS

Aders, Gebhard, *History of the German Night Fighter Force 1917-1945*, Jane's, London (1979)

Balke, Ulf, *Der Luftkrieg in Europa 1941-1945: Die Einsätze des Kampfgeschwaders 2 gegen England und über dem Deutschen Reich* (Teil 2), Bechtermünz Verlag, Augsburg (1997)

Beauvais, Heinrich, Kössler, Karl, Mayer, Max and Regel, Christoph, *German Secret Flight Test Centres to 1945*, Midland Publishing, Hinckley (2002)

Brown, Capt Eric, *Wings of the Luftwaffe*, Airlife Publishing, Shrewsbury (1979)

Butler, Phil, *War Prizes – An Illustrated survey of German, Italian and Japanese aircraft brought to Allied countries during and after the Second World War*, Midland Counties Publications, Leicester (1994)

Coates, Steve, with Carbonel, Jean-Christophe, *Helicopters of the Third Reich*, Classic Publications, Hersham (2002)

Forsyth, Robert, *Shadow over the Atlantic – Fernaufklärungsgruppe 5, The Luftwaffe and the U-boats: 1943–45*, Osprey Publishing, Oxford (2017)

Hentschel, Georg, *Die geheimen Konferenzen des Generalluftzeugmeisters: Ausgewählte und kommentierte Dokumente zur Geschichte der deustchen Luftrüstung und des Luftkrieges 1942-1944*, Bernard & Graefe Verlag, Koblenz (1989)

Hoffschmidt, Edward J., *German Aircraft Guns WW1-WW2*, WE Inc., Old Greenwich (1969)

Irving, David, *The Rise and Fall of the Luftwaffe – The Life of Erhard Milch*, Weidenfeld and Nicolson, London (1973)

Regnat, K. H., *Vom Original zum Modell: Dornier Do 335*, Bernard & Graefe Verlag, Bonn (1999)

Rys, Marek, *Dornier Do 335 Pfeil*, AJ Press, Gdansk (2000)

Smith, J. Richard, and Creek, Eddie J., *Dornier 335*, Monogram Aviation Publications, Boylston (1983)

Smith, J. Richard, and Creek, Eddie J., with Roletschek, Gerhard, *Do 335 Pfeil/Arrow*, Classic/Crecy Publishing, Manchester (2017)

WEBSITES

heiner-doerner-windenergie.de

luft46.com

deZeng IV, Henry L., and Stankey, Douglas G., *Luftwaffe Officer Career Summaries* at www.ww2.dk/lwoffz.html

INDEX